"I have been on tour for fifteen years and I now see that many top players are using Carl's methods. It was just a matter of time before his methods surfaced among the best players in the world."

—Gary Hallberg, PGA TOUR PLAYER

"I never had a teacher and I based all my early development on Carl's first book, *One Move to Better Golf.* To this day, I base my swing on setting up properly, and I think that it is paramount in Carl's new book."

—Fred Funk, PGA TOUR PLAYER

"Carl's clear and accurate principles have had a profound impact on my game and on my teaching. I offer instruction to players of all abilities. From the beginner all the way to Fred Couples, each is attempting a better execution and understanding of the golf swing. Because of Carl, I am able to execute and understand the swing to a much greater degree. I want to thank him for helping me become an infinitely better teacher!"

—Paul Marchand, FRED COUPLES'S
COACH AND PGA PROFESSIONAL,
HOUSTON COUNTRY CLUB

"Carl has put into words and illustrations some key theories that I can verify through research with my mechanical PING MAN."

—Karsten Solheim, FOUNDER AND
PRESIDENT OF KARSTEN
MANUFACTURING CORP.,
MAKER OF PING GOLF CLUBS

"I first met Carl Lohren in 1988 and instantly became impressed with his methods and ideas about the golf swing. Carl's ideas come from the most explosive era in golf— that is, from players like Ben Hogan and Sam Snead. His one-move theory was a big part of my success in capturing my second National Long Drive title in 1991."

—Art Sellinger, TWO-TIME WINNER
OF THE NATIONAL LONG DRIVE
CHAMPIONSHIP

"Years ago I went to see Carl Lohren for help with my swing, and what he had to say about moving the left shoulder to start the swing was a big key in helping me. He teaches the way Lee Trevino and Ray Floyd play."

—Larry Laoretti, PGA TOUR PLAYER

Getting Set for Golf

CARL LOHREN

WITH AL BARKOW

VIKING

VIKING
Published by the Penguin Group
Penguin Books USA Inc., 375 Hudson Street,
New York, New York 10014, U.S.A.
Penguin Books Ltd, 27 Wrights Lane,
London W8 5TZ, England
Penguin Books Australia Ltd, Ringwood,
Victoria, Australia
Penguin Books Canada Ltd, 10 Alcorn Avenue,
Toronto, Ontario, Canada M4V 3B2
Penguin Books (N.Z.) Ltd, 182–190 Wairau Road,
Auckland 10, New Zealand

Penguin Books Ltd, Registered Offices:
Harmondsworth, Middlesex, England

First published in 1995 by Viking Penguin,
a division of Penguin Books USA Inc.

10 9 8 7 6 5 4 3 2 1

LIBRARY OF CONGRESS CATALOGING IN PUBLICATION DATA
Lohren, Carl.
Getting set for golf/Carl Lohren with Al Barkow.
p. cm.
ISBN 0-670-85562-6
1. Swing (Golf). I. Barkow, Al. II. Title.
GV979.S9L62   1995
796.352'2—dc20   94-16357

This book is printed on acid-free paper.
∞
Printed in the United States of America
Set in ITC Century Light
Designed by Amy Hill

I want to dedicate this book to two people. First, my wife, Beryl. We have been married for thirty-four years, and I can honestly say that no man, and especially a golf professional, could have a more supportive and better wife. I love her dearly.

I also want to dedicate this book to Larry Fenster. Without Larry, this book would not exist. He has been my best friend for more than twenty years and has helped me in golf and in life. A man could not have a better friend.

Carl Lohren

Acknowledgments

The Lord Jesus Christ—Everything I have is through Him.

Ann Shulman, Tammy Lohren, and Holly Lohren, my daughters, all of whom play golf—Ann has been inspiring, loving, and analytical. Tammy has been a loving motivator. She holds a master's degree in exercise physiology, and has special insight into my teaching techniques. She is an expert teacher and has inspired me to continue to improve my methods. Holly has been inspiring, loving, and sensitive. Holly was also a great companion when she caddied for me on the PGA Senior Tour in 1990.

Al Barkow—Al believes in my material, and it is a real pleasure to have had him help me write this book. I consider him to be the best golf writer in the world. He is a good player and, more importantly, a good friend.

Deane Beman—Deane, one of the greatest golfers I've ever seen, has been a lifelong best friend. I cannot say enough for the support and help he has given me in many things.

Gene Borek—Gene has been a best friend for twenty-seven years. He is a PGA Master Professional, and in my opinion the best golf professional in America. He has also helped me in everything in life.

Babe Hiskey—Babe has been a best friend for twenty-four years. A fine tour player with several victories, he led me to Colonel Thieme's ministry, for which I will be eternally grateful. Babe has a lot of golf smarts. We travel together and always enjoy each other's company. Our families are very close.

Scott Shulman—My son-in-law, Scott, has been very supportive. I love him as though he were my son.

Col. R. B. Thieme, Jr.—His Bible teaching has been the cornerstone of my life and that of my family for twenty-three years.

Sue Morgan Marino—Sue has been an assistant to me for thirteen years, and is very knowledgeable about my technique. She has been a loyal help to me in many ways.

Harold and Betty Lohren—I want to thank my parents for their help and guidance, and for introducing me to golf. They sacrificed financially for my career in golf. I have great parents.

Rusty Jones—Rusty was great to work with. He is a fine illustrator, and as a golfer himself he caught exactly what I wanted to be shown.

North Shore C. C.—which was my home for thirty years.

Bill Strausbaugh, Jr.—a close friend who helped me in many ways, including introducing me to Irv Schloss.

Irv Schloss—who gave me Center, Radius, Plane, and Coil.

Foreword

Twenty-five years ago Carl Lohren revealed to me the *controlling* fundamentals of the golf swing in such a simple and understandable way that all the mysterious, interrelated parts that I had been struggling with for years were immediately put into their proper order and importance.

I've been privileged to have seen almost all the players and important shots played since the middle 1950s. Everything that I have observed about great golf shots convinces me that Carl possesses a unique and special knowledge about the golf swing.

Do you really want to improve your game? Do you thirst to know what to do? How to do it? And why? Let me give you an example of why the knowledge contained in this book and in Carl's first book, *One Move to Better Golf*, is worth any price to someone who is searching for the special feeling that comes from hitting a really good golf shot.

If you don't set up correctly, it is impossible to improve. *Impossible*.

When your shoulders are to the right of square at address, during the swing your automatic reflexes will reroute the club so that you start the ball toward (or left of) your intended target. The result is usually a weak slice. Sometimes your reflexes work a different way, and you actually make a good swing of the club from inside to out that hits the ball straight and true . . . and in the middle of the trees to the right. Does all this sound familiar?

This is a tough enough game as it is, and when your good swings produce bad shots (i.e., trees to the right), and your bad swings turn out relatively good ones (i.e., weak slices that limp down the fairway after curving over third base), it is just impossible to improve. Carl Lohren incorporates in this book all the fundamentals he has always taught, including the one move that initiates the swing. But his emphasis on the setup and proper shoulder and hip alignment at address is the bedrock of a repeating golf swing. Without correct alignment and setup, even if you make his one move, you would do well to spend most of your practice time chipping and putting . . . because you are going to need it.

I'll let Carl and Al Barkow take it from here. You are fortunate to have the most knowledgeable golf teacher in the game teamed with a golf-wise writer to unfold the mysteries of the golf swing in the pages that follow.

Good golf is worth all the hard work and frustration we all endure. If it came easily, it just wouldn't be as much fun or as gratifying when we succeed.

Good luck and good golfing.

Deane Beman
former commissioner, PGA Tour

Preface

Everything I said about making the golf swing in my first book, *One Move to Better Golf*, is still what I believe and continue to teach. But over the years I have refined certain aspects of the concept and expanded on it in what I believe are very important ways. One result of that growth in understanding and knowledge is a shift in emphasis. I have come to realize that the way a golfer sets up at the ball—his address position—is extremely important as to how he is going to make the swing itself. That may sound obvious, but in fact the address is given only cursory attention in much golf instruction. The setup determines or predetermines what shape the swing will have, how much power it will generate, the type of flight trajectory and degree of accuracy will be achieved. Thus, I now think of myself as a preswing teacher, not an inswing teacher. If the preswing is incorrect, the inswing will also be incorrect. It's as simple as that.

The preswing is vital, because the golf swing takes only a second and a half to complete. That is hardly enough time in which to make adjustments. This is even more the case with the forward swing, which is what I prefer to call the downswing. Anything going down is bound to go faster than something going up. The forward swing is a "happening," an event that must occur without any thought. Everything I teach about the golf swing comes before the forward swing, but is, of course, meant to make the forward swing effective.

Therefore, this book will deal at much greater length with addressing the ball than most instruction books do—what the setup positions should be, how to get into them, and what each means to the four fundamentals of the swing itself that I think are important. Those fundamentals are: Center, Radius, Plane, and Coil. There is no particular order to the four; they are really interdependent, but each needs to be dealt with separately. In the meantime, here are capsule definitions of each so that the discussion of the setup that begins this book will be meaningful.

Center—When the upper body turns at the start of the backswing, it does not move outside the space it occupied at address. It remains centered. This recalls the image of "swinging in a barrel" that Percy Boomer made popular in the 1940s. In the forward swing, your head remains where it was at address, while the rest of your body moves to the left as your weight shifts to that side.

Radius—It is from the left shoulder to the left hand. Extension of the radius refers to the path it takes.

Plane—The path the arms take in the backswing and forward swing. There is no one plane for all golfers. The plane depends on each individual's physical structure and how the address is taken. In any case, the plane changes during the transition from the backswing to the forward swing.

Coil—The rotation, or windup, of the *upper* body. The swing starts with the left shoulder and upper body moving *before* the lower body does. The lower body will eventually turn, but never as much as the upper body. If both parts move together, you don't get coil; you get a turn. Coiling loads the swing with power. It creates a slingshot effect. Turning does not.

.   .   .

This is the essential character of the golf swing I teach: The takeaway begins with the turn of the left shoulder. Your hands and arms swing and do not get closer to your body than they were at address. As the upper body coils, your hands and arms (and the club) raise up and move behind you. The plane now changes, because the lower part of your body moves toward the target. Your hands and club start down toward the ball from slightly under the backswing path and more inside the target line. At impact the clubhead is moving down the line of flight.

That is a concise, simplified description of the basic swing. There are details within the swing, to be sure, but as they are outlined, try to visualize the whole swing as often as you can.

I realize that the address position is essentially static and that people are more intrigued by, interested in, excited by the swing itself, because it hits the ball. And ball flight is what makes golf so fascinating a game. Still, it is important that you bear with me during the preswing section of the book. I will be relating each of the address positions to the actual swing action, which I think will help keep your interest. Have faith in my emphasis. I know very well that it means everything to effective golf.

I will also add an aspect of golf that was barely touched on in my earlier book, simply because then I didn't realize its importance. I am talking about ambidexterity, the ability to use both sides of your body in playing golf. The number of outstanding athletes in all sports who have some degree of ambidexterity is remarkable, so many that it undeniably has to do with their accomplishments. For the golf swing I teach it is especially useful to have ambidexterity. Everybody has some. You have some, but you may not know it. I will describe ways for you to assess your ambidexterity, and I will recommend exercises and drills that will increase your capacity to use both sides of your body to play better golf.

Carl Lohren

Contents

The Moment of Truth: Impact

I am beginning this book with the ending, because knowing your destination at the outset of a trip always makes the journey easier, less stressful. The positions you see in these illustrations of Ben Hogan and Lee Trevino at impact are where I am taking you. Everything I talk about is meant to bring you to these positions. You can achieve them. You may not look exactly like Trevino or Hogan, just as Trevino and Hogan don't look precisely alike, but that is only because everyone is built differently.

What is the central feature of the impact position that is our goal? It is a dominant left side and a corresponding collapsed or subjugated right side. (For left-handed golfers it is simply a matter of reversing the sides in this and all other aspects of this book.) Let me put it another way. The right *side* is delayed. One of the most common pieces of golf instruction is that the release of the right hand should be delayed as long as possible—kept from uncocking too soon in the forward swing. By itself, that is good instruction. You do want that delay. But it is very hard to do if you try to do it only with the hand. What I teach produces the delayed release by virtue of the address position I put you in, and the backswing that results from it. It is much easier to delay the whole right side than just the right hand. Delay the right side and the right hand will follow suit.

What are the details of the ideal impact position that can be seen in these illustrations? The left arm is straight, the right arm is bent. The right shoulder is down, the left shoulder is up. The left leg is braced, the right leg is collapsed. Everything about the right side is subjugated to a dominant left side. There are other things that you can't see but that are important to the action—such as where the club is held in the hands. The club must be held in the fingers of the right hand, and in the palm and fingers of the left hand. I will explain this grip completely in the chapter on the setup.

Delaying the right side solves one of the biggest problems in golf; that is, releasing or unhinging the right hand too soon—throwing the club from the top, or casting it, as we often say. This almost invariably brings the clubhead across the ball from outside to inside the target line, producing a shot either badly pulled to the left or, more often, sliced to the right.

The most effective golf is played with a dominant left side. Everything I teach is aimed at creating that. But it also requires a certain degree of ambidexterity. By that I mean coordination in your "unnatural" or opposite side. As I mentioned in my preface, I will be discussing ambidexterity in a separate chapter of this book, but before I do, I want to remind you whenever possible that it helps achieve the golf swing I teach.

For now, keep in mind that the central theme of this book is the creation of a dominant left side and a collapsed right side at impact.

CHAPTER ONE

The Preswing

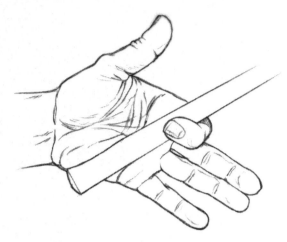

In the left hand the club handle runs diagonally from the middle crease of the index finger to beneath the heel pad. It is important that the club be *under* the heel pad.

The left-hand grip is completed when the last three fingers wrap around the handle, the main contact being at the juncture of the fingers and palm. This creates a combination finger-and-palm hold that will be very secure without your having to hold the club tightly.

The left thumb runs down the right center of the handle.

The Grip

A correct grip is extremely important to every aspect of the golf swing and goes a long way toward keeping the right hand and side from being dominant in the swing. I will start with the left hand, because it is the first to go on the club.

THE LEFT HAND

The handle should run on a diagonal line from the middle crease of the index finger to beneath the heel pad. The left thumb runs along the top of the handle but not down the very center. It should be slightly right of center. The pressure of the last three fingers on the handle and the placement of the club underneath the bottom of the heel pad firms the left forearm and maintains control of the club without the necessity to grip it tightly. The club is now secure, and the left hand as a whole is more dominant than the right hand, because it uses a combination of the hand *and* the fingers to hold it.

The right hand makes its connection with the left hand by fitting the little finger around the knuckle of the left index finger. This is known as the Vardon Overlapping Grip. Its greatest value is that it keeps the right hand from being too dominant, because the right hand holds the left thumb and takes orders from the left hand.

THE RIGHT HAND AND ITS CONNECTION

This part of the grip is especially crucial to success. It is essentially a finger-oriented hold, but before detailing the finger positions I want to discuss how the right hand should be connected to the left. I strongly recommend the Vardon Overlapping Grip in which the little finger of the right hand fits around behind the knuckle of the left index finger, or on top of it piggyback style. I recommend this not for the reason most often given—that it helps the hands work together in the swing—but because it keeps the right hand from being dominant. With a "baseball grip," one of two other basic grips, all the fingers of the right hand are on the handle and the right hand has too much influence in the swing.

The other commonly used connection that I also discourage is the Interlocking Grip, in which the right hand's little finger intertwines with the index finger of the left hand. I see many new golfers interlocking, on the premise that they have short fingers. But I think the fact that Jack Nicklaus interlocks may have more to do with it. In any case, the Interlocking Grip makes you feel that the sureness of the grip depends on this connec-

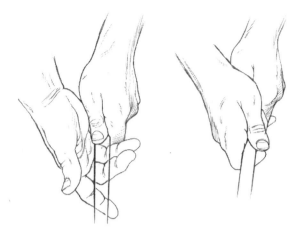

Hold the club with the fingers of the right hand rather than the palm, for greater feel of the clubhead and left-hand domination.

When the right hand is closed to complete the grip, its lifeline should be at the side of the handle, and the hollow of the hand should cover the left thumb.

tion. Also, even when done correctly, I believe it tenses the underside of the right arm. The tendency, then, is to use too much of the index finger to interlock with. This pushes the right hand too deeply down so that the club is held in the palm. This also gives the right hand too much influence in the swing.

As for placement of the right-hand fingers, imagine that the handle of the club is square rather than round so we can say it has a top, bottom, and two sides. The bottom pad of the middle and third fingers is underneath the handle—on the bottom. The middle crease of the index finger is on the right side of the handle. Depending on the length of your fingers, the tip of the right index finger may or may not touch the handle. It is not important if it doesn't, and if you try to make it do so, the right hand may be pulled too much under the handle. When you close the right hand, the hollow or valley between the heel pad and thumb pad should be against the right side of and covering the left thumb. Only the inside edge of the right thumb touches the handle.

The twist or angle of each hand in relation to the shaft depends on how your hands hang from your sides when you're standing naturally, not in the shoulders-back military-attention way. Putting it on a numerical basis, a palm parallel to your side is a One. If turned to the right or left a few degrees, it's a Two; a little more turn, it's a Three. A little more a Four. If the back of a hand is facing in front of you, it's a Five. For most people, each hand is a Two, Three, or Four. Whatever it is, that is the degree of twist each should have on the handle. Why? Because the hands, under the pressure generated during the golf swing, will instinctively return to their most comfortable, natural angle. This change occurring during the swing will almost invariably bring a poor shot. Only a natural Five, which is very rare, will have to be rearranged at address to a Three or Four.

If the left hand is too "strong"—twisted too far to the right—the left shoulder is lifted too much or hunched at address. Your left arm may swing back, but your upper trunk won't coil. If the right hand is too "high"—twisted too much to the left—your right shoulder probably won't be low enough at address. And the hand will be less apt to roll to the right or supinate in the backswing. The plane will be too vertical, and maximum radius is not attained.

To repeat, by holding the club in the palm of the right hand you create strength in the right hand and arm. This in turn makes the entire right side of the body too dominant. By connecting the hands with the Vardon Overlapping Grip and keeping the right thumb and forefinger on the handle as I've described above, you de-arm the right side. Grip pressure then doesn't matter much, although in general I recommend a fairly light hold in both hands because the hands will tighten instinctively as you begin your swing. In some cases, if you hold the club very tightly to begin with, you will develop too much tension throughout your body and you won't be able to move your big muscles effectively.

The E O L Formula

I have developed a formula—E O L—that highlights the three most important basic positions of the body at address. E is for Erectness, O for Open shoulders and hips, L for the Left shoulder being higher than the right shoulder. They are very much interrelated, and all must be as described in the following sections.

E = ERECTNESS, OR POSTURE

At address there are two angles to the spine in respect to erectness, which is the word I prefer for posture. One is at the top of the spine, the short distance from the shoulder blades up to the top of the spinal column, what I refer to as "between the shoulders." You can see it clearly in

Jack Nicklaus (left) and Tom Purtzer are excellent examples of proper erectness at address. The bend of the main spine—from the waist to the shoulder blades—is in the area of 20 to 30 degrees. From the shoulder blades up to between the shoulders, the bend is between 70 and 80 degrees.

Jack Nicklaus, who has a kind of buffalo hump in that area. The bend here could be as much as 90 degrees, although in most cases it will be around 70 or 80 degrees.

The other area of the spine is from the shoulder blades down to the sacroiliac, what I call the "main spine." It is most important to good posture. If the main spine is too erect, the shoulders won't tilt and turn correctly in the backswing. Your arms will move inside too quickly, and the swing will get too flat too early—it will be beneath your correct plane. A lot of golfers with long arms make this error.

Or, because the spine is too erect and the shoulder turn too level, the lower body moves at the same time as the upper body and you do not achieve a proper coil. To get the upper body moving (and coiling) before the lower body, the upper body has to be bent forward between 20 and 30 degrees.

By the same token, if you are hunched over with the main spine bent more than 30 degrees forward, your left shoulder could dip too low in the takeaway and create too vertical a swing plane. And the radius will be shortened. Also, your right hip will jut out to the right. This is better known as a "sway." Whatever term is used, what happens is that you lose your center.

O = OPENED SHOULDERS AND HIPS

In the address position commonly taught, there is an imaginary line from the clubface to the target—called the target line—and imaginary lines across the shoulders, hips, and feet that are approximately parallel to the target line. For the setup I teach, the feet are parallel to the target line, but

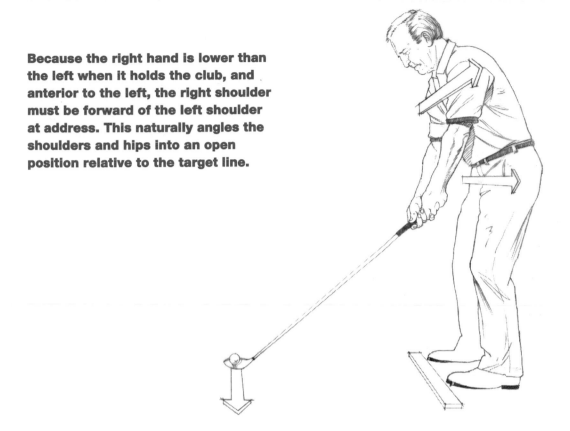

Because the right hand is lower than the left when it holds the club, and anterior to the left, the right shoulder must be forward of the left shoulder at address. This naturally angles the shoulders and hips into an open position relative to the target line.

the shoulders and hips are not. This is a significant difference, and is at the heart of my system. The shoulders and hips are open. That is, the imaginary line running through the shoulders is about 20 degrees left of the parallel line, the one through the hips about 15 degrees left. Some golf teachers and players think this is unusual, idiosyncratic, radical. But I didn't invent this. I noticed it on many great golfers, and particularly on the two I have the most respect for as ballstrikers, Ben Hogan and Lee Trevino.

There is a physiological reason for the shoulders being open. The golf club lies on an oblique angle from you at address, and your right hand is anteriorly lower on the handle than the left. Therefore, the right shoulder *must* be slightly forward of the left shoulder. You can't argue with

Ben Hogan at address, his shoulders and hips open. You can tell he is open because you can't see any part of his left arm from this down-the-target-line perspective. This is a checkpoint to use when you look at your address in a mirror or with a video camera from the same angle.

that. Forcing the right shoulder (and hips) back to be even with the left is unnatural.

Playing with an open shoulder (and hip) line refutes a couple of age-old golf instructions—"Keep the right elbow in close to your body," and, "The way you are at address is the way you want to be at impact." Both have no merit whatsoever. If you allow your shoulders to be open, the right elbow will be farther from your body than the left elbow. There is nothing wrong with that when you make the swing I teach. And it is virtually impossible for the address and impact position to be the same because in the forward swing there is a distinct weight shift to the left side and a turn of the hips. Therefore, the address position cannot be mimicked at impact if you make a proper swing.

How does the open shoulder and hip affect your center and help maintain it? The answer is in what usually happens if you pull the right shoulder back and square your shoulders at address, which most golfers are told to do. At the start of any golf swing, the left shoulder goes down and the right shoulder goes up. That's what makes the club go up in the air. But then the left shoulder moves laterally. Shoulders squared at address (or even worse, aimed to the right of the target in a closed position) are in effect already turned to the right. When the swing begins, they turn even more and the upper body sways laterally to the right. When you sway, you lose your center.

Or if the left shoulder is not higher at address than the right shoulder, it is less likely to descend when the backswing begins. It only moves laterally and, again, moves you off your center. You might also reverse-pivot, which I will explain in the chapter devoted to the backswing. For now, keep in mind that it is very difficult to return consistently to impact in a strong hitting position when you move off your center at the start of the swing. The shoulders and hips being open at address facilitate starting the backswing with the left shoulder, which blocks the possibility of a sway.

Open shoulders and hips help create a good radius or extension, because your hands are less likely to move closer to your body at the start of the takeaway. Golfers who start the club back to the inside of the target line, with their hands moving closer to their body, are likely to throw their right shoulder outward in the downswing in order to get the club moving down the line of flight. This in-and-over swing path is a right-side-dominant action.

The open shoulder and hip line at address is helpful in producing a good coil, because it makes the upper body *want* to activate the big muscles in your upper body with a full turn to the right. Along with producing a good coil, because the shoulders start their turn and leave the hips behind, momentarily a tug-of-war is created between the upper and lower body. The upper body wins the backswing, the lower body wins the forward swing. Which is as it should be.

One way to check if your shoulders and hips are open at address is with a mirror or video camera, looking as if you were behind yourself and looking down the target line. You should see only the under part of your left forearm. Looking at yourself from the front view (above), you should see part of your right shoulder sticking out past your left shoulder.

Fred Couples, Laura Davies, and Chi-Chi Rodriguez are noted for excellent upper-body coiling in the backswing, which results from being open with their shoulders and hips at address.

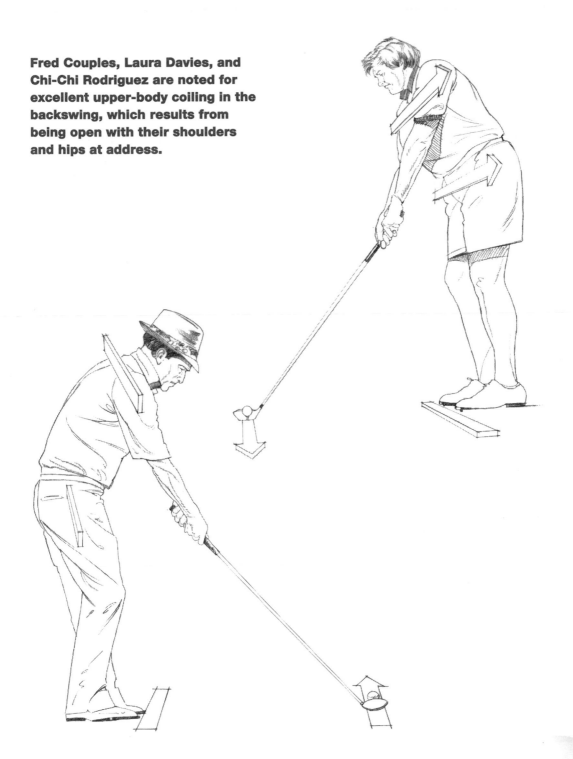

L=LEFT SHOULDER HIGHER THAN THE RIGHT

The formula headlines the left shoulder, but in fact the reason for its being higher is to make sure the right side is not dominant. The difference in height should be about six inches. The reason the right shoulder must be lower is to relax the trunk muscles in the upper right side (the pectoral and latissimus areas). This then facilitates four things: (1) You have the ability to turn the left shoulder at the start of the swing and contract the upper and middle back muscles on the left side. (2) The right arm is de-armed, made subordinate to the left side. (3) The spine is put right of center in relation to the spread of your feet. This is very important. (4) The right shoulder, being lower, allows the left shoulder to tilt automatically at the start of the backswing so the arms can raise as the swing progresses.

It is very important to a sound address that the left shoulder be higher than the right shoulder. The difference should be, on average, six inches. The position relaxes the muscles in the upper right side, which effectively allows the left side to be more dominant throughout the swing.

Jack Nicklaus and Lee Trevino have an almost exaggerated lower-right-shoulder/higher-left-shoulder setup. The position also inspires a turn of the left shoulder to start the backswing.

Getting into the Stance

For the sake of consistency and the mental comfort it brings under pressure, you should set up in your address position using the same routine every time. I developed my setup procedure after watching Arnold Palmer at a PGA Tour event in Maryland a number of years ago. What he did looked different to me at the time, and I thought about it a lot. It has since become the cornerstone of my teaching of the setup.

I noticed that when Palmer first stood up to the ball, putting the clubface directly behind it and aimed at the target, the butt end of the club was very close to his body. Also, his arms hung almost straight down and were also very close to his body. Eventually I realized that, among other things, his close proximity to the ball produced good posture because he did not have to bend at the waist to reach the ball with his club. He was using only shoulder tilt. If he had bent from the waist, he might not have gotten the left shoulder higher than the right. At the same time it got him aimed correctly. Also, when he moved back into his final hitting position he was always standing the right distance from the ball, no matter what club he was using, because he used the length of the club as the measure by which to take his stance. Finally, this makes it easier to get the shoulders and hips open.

Now let's go through the entire procedure for taking your stance. Begin with your left hand on the club in the correct position. From a point slightly behind the ball, and with your chest facing the target at about a 40-degree angle, take a short step with your right foot to where you can put the center of the clubface behind the ball with the butt end of the club very close to and just left of the center of your pelvis. Your weight is entirely on the right foot—the *whole* foot—not on the toes or heels. Your

Start getting into your stance from slightly behind the ball and facing the target at about a 40-degree angle. Your shoulders are level. Your right foot is closer to the ball than the left foot, but the left foot carries most of your weight. The club is held only in the left hand at this time.

Take a little step forward with your right foot and simultaneously put your right hand on the club as it goes behind the ball. Your left knee should bend and your left hip should move forward a little. Your right leg should be straight but not locked as it receives the weight shifted onto it.

The Preswing **35**

right leg is straight but not locked, and your left knee and hip move a little forward to release weight to the right and to keep your hips under your shoulders. At the same time that you have taken this little step, and while your body is moving forward and your left hand is moving the club to behind the ball, greet the club with your right hand going on the handle in the correct position. Your hands actually come across your body toward each other and meet at the pelvis. The idea is that they have moved an equal distance so the shoulders have not changed their openness. These movements should be simultaneous—and they will be, once you have done it a few times—so there is a nice rhythmic flow of motion rather than a stiff, robotic one.

Your right foot is closer to the ball than it will be when you are ready to hit it. Be sure the step to the ball is short, maybe three to five inches, and your left leg is gently flexed so you don't have to bend at the waist to reach it. Your right hip should be under you—on a line directly under your upper body and over your right knee. I call this being in torso alignment—the knee, hip, and upper torso on a line with one another. You lower yourself to the ball *first* with a tilt of your shoulders. Only while you are stepping back to complete your stance do you bend at the waist—about 20 degrees—and flex your knees. The best thing about this torso alignment is that it assures that *you will have the same posture with every club in the bag, and for every type of lie*. This in turn will let you make the same body turn and swing with all clubs and for all lies.

With the clubface behind the ball and the butt of the club near your pelvis, move the left foot up into the correct position relative to the ball and the target line. *The left foot must never go farther forward than or ahead of the right foot.* If the left foot moves forward of the right, you will end up in a closed address position, aiming your body to the right of your target. The left foot sets the distance you will stand from the ball, and the ball placement between your feet.

Next bring your right foot back into its final, correct position, setting it even with the left foot. Both feet (actually, the toes) should now be on the same line and parallel to the target line. Most importantly, when you bring the right foot back into its final position *the line of your shoulders and hips will be angled farther left than your feet*. The shoulders should be angled about 20 degrees left of the parallel line, the hips about 15 degrees. They are "open," and must remain that way.

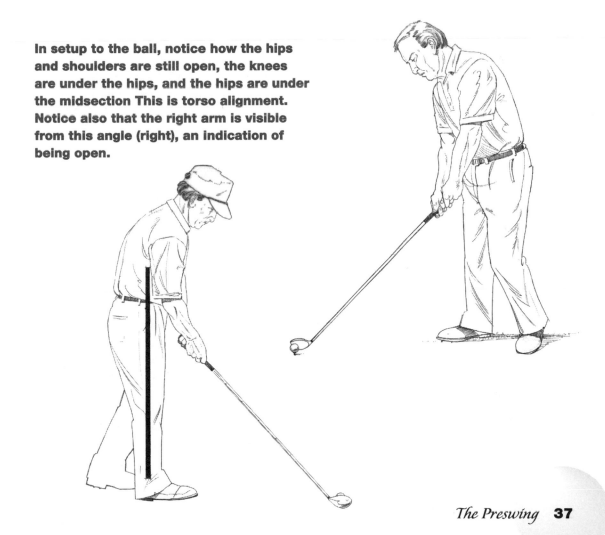

In setup to the ball, notice how the hips and shoulders are still open, the knees are under the hips, and the hips are under the midsection This is torso alignment. Notice also that the right arm is visible from this angle (right), an indication of being open.

The stance is now complete. Weight distribution is even on both legs and also evenly distributed along the full length of each foot. The hips are now back in the athletic position, there is no tension in the arms, and there has been no increase in the angle or bend of the upper spine. The left foot has been moved forward, but not as far forward as the right foot, which has been pulled back even with the left foot. Notice that the shoulders are now 20 degrees open, the hips 15 degrees open, which happens naturally when completing the stance.

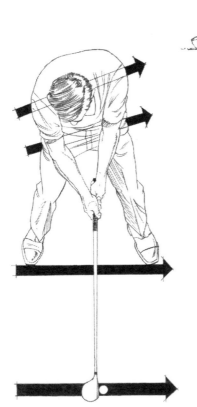

Left: In this view of the complete setup you can clearly see all the "open" elements in place. The clubface is aimed directly at the target and the feet are essentially perpendicular to the target line, but the shoulders are angled about 20 degrees left of the parallel line, the hips about 15 degrees.

WIDTH OF STANCE

I like the feet to be fairly wide apart at address—with the driver about the width of your shoulders measured from the insides of the feet, and somewhat narrower with the shorter clubs. This promotes lateral stability—a certain resistance against movement of the lower body—which induces an earlier coil and greater extension without losing your center. Experiment to find the width of stance for every club in the bag that will discourage an excess amount of lower body movement. Nobody is perfect, and sometimes the lower body will move a little too soon. But as a general rule, the width of your stance acts as a guard against too much lower body movement in the backswing.

DISTRIBUTION OF WEIGHT

Weight distribution on the legs is fifty-fifty. I don't believe in having more weight on one side or the other. Put more weight on the left than on the right leg and you will probably reverse-pivot—have your weight on your left side at the top of your backswing, and on your right side at impact. Place too much weight on the right side at address and you will not get a sufficient shift of weight to the left in the forward swing; you will stay back and hit behind the ball. Also, uneven weight distribution hampers the urge to produce sufficient body rotation.

Your weight should also be distributed evenly along the full length of your feet, from the heels to the toes. Too much weight backward on the heels or forward on the toes restricts your ability to turn, and you lose balance. A test of your balance is to take your stance and then have someone try to push you backward or forward. If you can't be easily pushed out of position either way, you have correct weight distribution.

BALANCE

The distribution of weight as described above will give you good balance at address. But each E O L element also affects balance at address, as well as during the swing. If you don't have E(rectness), you could fall forward during the takeaway. If you are not O(pen), you will swing the club back to the inside and up, and on the forward swing bring it from outside to inside the target line and fall forward. Without L(eft shoulder higher than the right), your right side is too dominant. When the swing begins, you will tip your head to the left, reverse-pivot, and be off balance to the left because the right side has elevated too quickly. Or because your right shoulder is too high, your right arm could be hyperextended and you will pull yourself to the right and be off balance to that side.

However, good preswing balance through weight distribution does not assure good inswing balance. Staying centered in the backswing, which is a lack of movement sideways, up and down or forward and backward, is the result of turning correctly.

There are other aspects of balance. For instance, if you are right-eye dominant, but for some reason tilt your head to the right at address and look at the ball primarily with your left eye (perhaps because you see Jack Nicklaus doing that), you will be doing something unnatural and lose your equilibrium; you will not have a good sense of balance during the swing, and you will lose your center.

Also, as you waggle the club in preparation for beginning the stroke (see the sidebar in Chapter Two), you should also move your feet alternately in place. Lift the entire foot up and down, not just the heel or toe. If you raise and lower only the toes—wiggle them—you will be off balance to the rear. If you raise and lower only the heels, you will be off balance forward. If you can alternately lift each foot and put it down, you *have* to be on balance. This also creates motion that helps alleviate tension. The swing will be easier to start; it will just flow.

BALL PLACEMENT

The ball is always placed somewhere between your feet, of course, but never right of center. Generally, the ball is placed more toward the left heel as club length increases. To cover the parameters: with the driver, the ball is on a line with the inside of the left heel; with the nine-iron and wedges, in the center of your stance. If you have the ball right of center or too far back, you will get your right shoulder even with or behind the left shoulder; you won't be open, and the club will start back on the inside with the hands moving closer to your body.

If the ball is set too far forward, beyond the left heel, your right shoulder will be too far forward. If you are going to err in ball placement, err to the left or more forward; but ball placement is easily controlled and shouldn't be a problem. Once these parameters are learned, ball placement should be left to your instincts.

AIMING

I've been told that the way I teach aiming in golf is unique. Well, it is much different than any other aiming instruction that I have ever come across. My method of aiming is designed to ease the mind, because aiming can be a very tension-creating element in golf. Many golfers, including the best professionals, get hung up on aiming; you see them twisting their body and the clubface around nervously until they are finally aimed correctly, or think they are. My idea is to rely on subconscious instincts to get properly aimed. My good friend Gene Borek said to me after he learned my system that it worked the first time he tried it and it has worked every time thereafter.

Here's how it works. Start from behind your ball, looking toward the target. Don't look casually at the target; instead, burn it into your mind and your mind's eye. Really get a good look at it, because *you are never going to look at it again.* Then move up to the ball and into the address position. It is very important that you be 45 degrees open when you step up to the ball. If you begin to get into the address position with your entire body parallel to the target line, you will only be using one of your eyes to aim at your target. With both eyes working and the clubface square in your hands, you will aim your clubface squarely at your target. You will also align your body and arrange your feet correctly to the position of the clubface. I challenge anybody who says this will not happen.

When people ask me what is the rationale for this system of aiming, I respond: Watch a third baseman who has gone to his left to grab a grounder. He turns and throws to first without first looking at his target. Or, watch a basketball player going to his right get a quick shot off to his left and score. Same thing. They can do this because they *know* where the target is; it has been burned into their brain, into their mind's eye, and they react to it instinctively. Do you have to be a trained athlete to do this? Not at all. I get beginner golfers to aim correctly by my system after one lesson. It doesn't take a trained sense, just natural sense. To prove my point to students, to show them that it works, I tell them to look at me very closely to see where I am standing, then walk about four feet away with their back to me and a golf ball in their hand. I then tell them to throw the golf ball over their shoulder or head to where they remember I am. Every time, they throw the ball right at me. If a person can do that, then he or she can put the clubhead down with its face aimed at the target without any fussing.

Once you are set over the ball, you don't have to look at the target again. Watch Lee Trevino, Chi-Chi Rodriguez, or Larry Mize and you will see that they seldom, if ever, look at the target after they get set up to the ball.

The point is that the act of aiming can create psychological tension. The tension gets in the way of clearing your mind of all thoughts during your preswing routine and blocks the only thought you should have as you start the swing—the turn of the left shoulder. Just burn the target into your mind for three or four seconds, then set up to the ball. You will be aimed correctly.

A RECAP OF THE SETUP

I want to put the total picture of the setup before you. This is how you should be at the ball when you're ready to hit it.

- The clubface is aimed directly at the target.
- Your feet are nearly perpendicular to the target line.

- Weight distribution is equal on each leg and along the full length of each foot.
- Your shoulders are angled open about 20 degrees left of the parallel line; your hips are angled open about 15 degrees.
- Your right shoulder is approximately six inches lower than your left shoulder.
- The flex at the hips is about 20 degrees; that is, from the base of your spine up to your shoulder blades. From the shoulder blades up to the top of your spine, you are bent anywhere from 70 to 90 degrees.
- Your knees are slightly flexed.
- Your buttocks jut out a little behind you.

It seems like a lot on the written page, but once you have practiced this routine, and used it in regular play on the course, it will take you two or three seconds to get into position. The routine accomplishes everything.

AN EXTRA MEASURE FOR GETTING INTO THE STANCE

For golfers who can accept more detailed technique, there is another step in the procedure for getting into the stance that further assures a sound position at the ball. It is an add-on to the method described in the main text of this chapter. I call it measuring. It comes *before* putting the clubhead behind the ball.

Begin by holding the club in the right hand and walking naturally up to the ball, stopping with the right foot a little ahead of the left foot (about four inches). Simultaneously place the clubhead on the ground one and a half to two inches from the ball. As you set the club down, take your left-hand grip. About 98 percent of your weight is on your right leg, and your upper body is more or less parallel to the target line. Your shoulders are level. The butt of the club is very close to your body, and your left arm is extended down its full length and just opposite your pelvis.

Now step back an inch or so with both feet, bringing the club back with you, and take your right hand off the handle. While doing this, half-face the target with your shoulders level. Immediately step forward again with the right foot and place the clubhead behind the ball while you take your correct right-hand grip. You should be in alignment as previously explained and illustrated, and be 35 degrees open. Next, move your left foot up so the toes are a little past the center of the right foot.

Bring the right foot back into its final position with your hips flexed and knees bent slightly. Your shoulders are now 20 degrees open, your hips 15 degrees open. You are now set to swing.

The purpose of the measuring is to insure that the step you make to put the clubhead behind the ball is a short one. This allows you to shift your weight and be in torso alignment. This will give you E O L.

CHAPTER TWO

The Full Swing

The Backswing—
The First Move
Is the One

The most effective golf swing is a left-side-dominant action, with the right side passive. It stands to reason, then, that everything possible should be done to have the left side in control at all times. That is not as easy as it sounds, because most right-handed golfers are also right-side dominant—they brush their teeth, hold a glass, write their name with their right hand. Chapter Three is about ambidexterity, and in it I will deal at length with how my system for setting up to the ball and swinging at it produces effective ambidexterity. For now I only want to explain how the backswing starts. It is the mainspring of my system, for it triggers all that follows.

The golf swing begins with a turn of the left shoulder. Why the left shoulder? Because there has to be a simultaneous upper body turn and arm swing at the start of the golf swing, and the left shoulder is the only part of the anatomy connected to both. Thus the unified action. Furthermore, this insures that the left arm is (and creates) the radius of the swing. The left shoulder turns forward, and then goes laterally to the right. It is a continuous, flowing movement. The arms and hands move

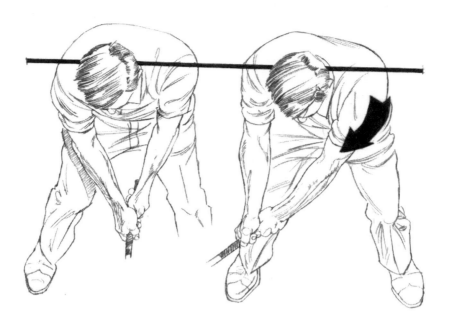

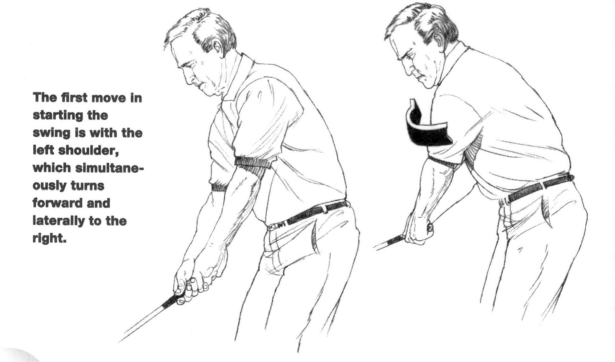

The first move in starting the swing is with the left shoulder, which simultaneously turns forward and laterally to the right.

Fred Couples perfectly demonstrates the first move, especially in being dead still from the waist down.

with the shoulder and remain in the same extended positions they were in before the swing began. Actually, because of their swinging motion, which the turning of the left shoulder helps to initiate, the arms help pull the shoulders around. As I've said, all the individual movements of the golf swing are interdependent.

Here is how my Four Fundamentals result from this single move.

STAYING CENTERED

Staying centered means that in the backswing the body stays within the space it occupied at address. Imagine it another way: Your upper body is

Again Fred Couples illustrates a key element of the system and shows what staying centered means and looks like. (Let me add here that I have never worked with or discussed the golf swing I teach with Fred Couples, Jack Nicklaus, Lee Trevino, Ben Hogan, or any other players used as examples in this book. That they do the things I teach is a reflection of where I have obtained many of my ideas, and why I believe these ideas are cornerstones of good golf.)

in a box. When you turn it, it does not touch the four sides or the top. There is no up-and-down, forward-and-backward, or side-to-side movement. There is just a coiling.

You don't have to move laterally to shift weight, as so much instruction implies. In fact, you must not. If the body moves sideways, or laterally, that is called a sway. A sway does not allow for the building of a powerful windup of the upper body. And in the forward swing you will invariably sway in the opposite direction, a right-side-dominant action that burns up power before it is needed and produces inaccurate shots.

By staying centered, you will be able consistently to return the club-face to the ball with the face square to the target line, and with the stability that brings maximum power.

Starting the backswing with the turn of the left shoulder insures that you will remain centered, because your right side will necessarily go backward at the same time, as the sides are connected through the union of the hands on the handle of the club. Lateral movement cannot occur.

DEVELOPING THE RADIUS

The radius of your swing is determined by the length of your left arm from the shoulder to the fingertips. As long as the right side of your body stays passive and your left arm remains comfortably extended during the swing, you will produce the longest or widest possible arc. The right arm cannot be the radius, because it must bend midway through the backswing, which shortens its length. The left arm will remain extended if you begin the backswing with the left shoulder and keep the right arm passive.

Remember, you want your hands and the club still going back when the lower body begins moving forward. An extension of the radius means your hands either stay the same distance from your body or get a little farther out from it at the beginning of the backswing. The longer and

Fred Couples and Lee Trevino display the key to making a good radius, their hands never getting closer to the body in the takeaway.

wider the backswing arc or radius is, the more time is borrowed to get coiled and for the lower body to begin its forward motion before the hands get to the apex of the backswing. Beginning the swing with the turn of the left shoulder insures this wide arc, because it keeps the hands, especially the right hand, and the right side passive in the swing. If you don't start with your left shoulder, you almost surely will with your hands, because they are holding the club—it is an instinct that the left-shoulder move deters.

The hands, being light in weight and controlled by small muscles, move very quickly. They want to be active when they are hitting something with a stick. That, too, is pure instinct, but the death of good golf.

Those quick-moving hands don't want to wait very long to get at hitting. Give them a chance and they will sling the club at the ball right from the top of the backswing. This dissipates any power that has been built up with the body turn and exaggerates the slicer's path to the ball already produced by the outside-to-in swing path.

By contrast, the left shoulder is big, heavy muscle and bone that moves surely. It has a certain skeletal structure that limits its range of

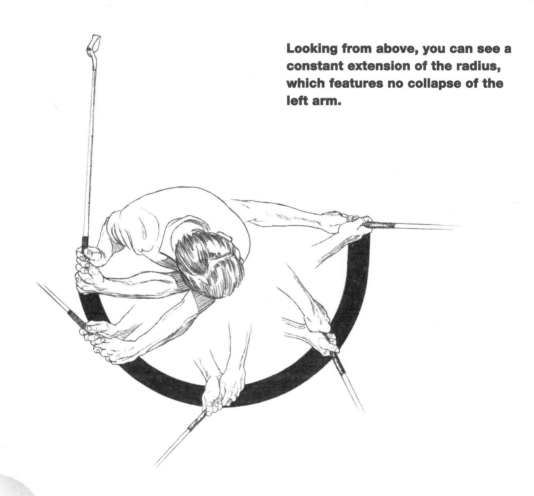

Looking from above, you can see a constant extension of the radius, which features no collapse of the left arm.

motion. There will be little deviation in the motion it is told to take. It is far more reliable in this respect than the hands. The left shoulder is like the hub of a wagon wheel; the hands (and arms and golf club) are the spokes and rim. By initiating the swing with the left shoulder, the hands are kept in their place as subordinates to the golf shot.

I don't mean to imply that the hands and arms have nothing to do with the swing. Although relatively passive, they do help pull the shoulders around. But if they start before the shoulders, the shoulders will not have enough time to make their full turn before the arms and hands begin to swing the club down to impact. If you are right-side dominant, it is necessary not only to start the swing with the turn of the left shoulder but to *think* of doing so because (1) it insures the movement will be made, and (2) it subjugates the right side in the takeaway, a step that goes a long way toward making you ambidextrous. It is almost impossible for the left side to dominate without a left-side *thought*, if you are right-handed. An overactive right side in the takeaway pulls the hands closer to the body and shrinks the radius.

GETTING ON PLANE

The plane is a by-product of your radius and center and is determined by your address. If you stand erect with the main part of your spine tilted from 20 to 30 degrees forward from perpendicular and begin the swing with the left shoulder, the plane will effectively establish itself. You don't consciously put the club on plane.

Think of the plane as an imaginary line drawn from the toe of the club up over your right shoulder, or, as a pane of glass leaning on that same

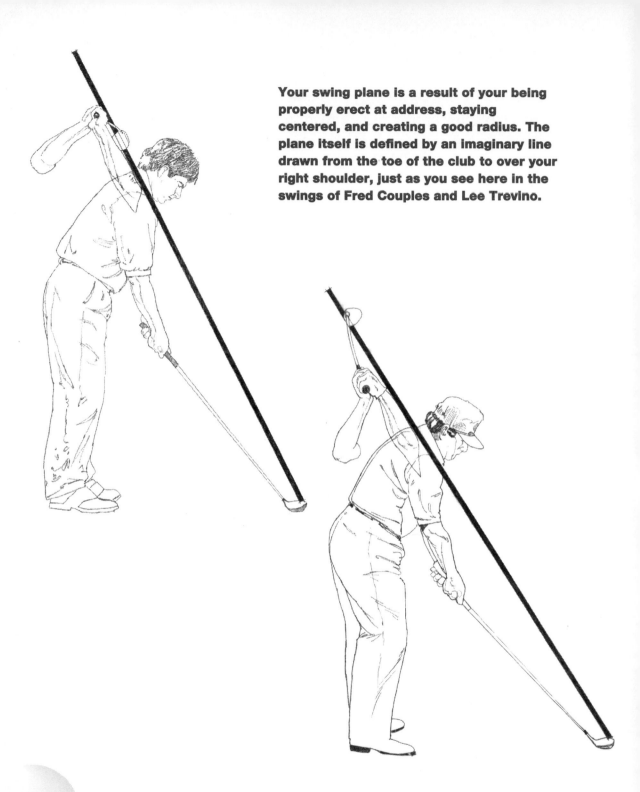

Your swing plane is a result of your being properly erect at address, staying centered, and creating a good radius. The plane itself is defined by an imaginary line drawn from the toe of the club to over your right shoulder, just as you see here in the swings of Fred Couples and Lee Trevino.

line. Your left hand gets on that plane at a certain point early in the backswing and rides up the plane to the top of the backswing. In the forward swing the left hand and clubhead move inside the pane of glass as your right shoulder drops down with the forward thrust of the lower body. The forward swing plane is thus a little flatter than the backswing plane. Trying to make this inswing adjustment or any other is almost impossible in the brief second that it takes to make the forward swing, and will produce only poor shots.

Turning the left shoulder first to start the backswing puts the club on the correct plane, because it prevents the body or arms from throwing the club and your hands to the inside, shortening the extension of the radius and producing slack. Staying centered and maintaining your radius further helps establish the plane of the swing. They are interdependent.

One more thing. You have to have enough centrifugal force established at the beginning of the swing to have the arms, hands, and club whirling or you won't create a plane. I will talk more about this later, in the section on tempo.

COIL FOR POWER

The main purpose of the coil or windup of the upper body in the backswing is the creation of a correct forward swing. Only if you coil will you develop the tension that forces the lower body to begin driving forward before the hands and the club reach the top of the backswing. What's more, the coil effectively keeps the other three fundamentals intact during the forward swing. You stay centered with your neck and head, and on plane with the radius remaining constant.

Nick Price and Gary Player exemplify the coil as it should be, by a turning of the upper body.

As I've pointed out, the coil is the rotation of the upper body to the right that begins before the lower body moves. The lower body moves only because the upper body moves it. You can't help but coil if you start the swing with the left shoulder, so you needn't think about it. If you consciously try to force a lot of coil, you will pull yourself out of your center. You will overturn and spoil the relationship between the upper and lower body. Just continue coiling until your body says enough. You will feel tension or tightening—what is better called loading—in the left latissimus muscle of your back. By the time you feel that loading, there is so much tension that something has to give. It's your lower body that will give, because it hasn't turned as much as the upper body and *because the hands and arms are still going back*. Your lower body will begin to move forward, but you don't do anything about that, either. You are, in effect, on automatic.

From this lower-body perspective of Davis Love III, you can see that there is no movement until the upper-body coil has pulled it.

I have intimated often that no thinking should be involved in the golf swing except the starting thought. I don't mean to say that the game is so easy with my swing system that you become a kind of robot. It is just that the swing I teach—or any other, for that matter—is of such short duration that there is no time to think about it. If you try, you will make a bad swing worse and a good one less effective.

All of which serves to emphasize further how important the preswing is.

In these illustrations of Fred Couples's back-swing coil you can see the left latissimus muscles gradually stretching or loading up as the club gets all the way to the top. Just as important, you see there is only a little tension in the right latissimus muscles.

The Waggle

Every golfer instinctively moves the club one way or the other while in the address position, and moments before beginning the swing itself. It's called the waggle, and it is a good way to keep from being too static or frozen at address. But for the waggle to be fully valuable it must be done a certain way. It should preview the rotation of the arms and hands that naturally occurs midway into the backswing

In this miniature version of the backswing, the left arm and hand pronate (the palm and forearm turn downward), and the right arm and hand supinate (the palm and forearm turn upward) as the club moves back a few feet. Both then turn back the other way (supinate and pronate, respectively) when bringing the clubhead back to the ball. The clubface will go from square to open, then back to square.

If you are gripping the club correctly in the left hand, and your right shoulder is lower than your left, this waggle helps promote left-side dominance in the swing.

If the shoulders are open, the waggle will go back and forth on the target line. *The shoulders should not be involved in the waggle.*

Another form of waggle is to lift your feet alternately up and down as you waggle the club and get your body set. As I mentioned in the section on balance, do not lift only the heel or toe of each foot, but the whole foot each time.

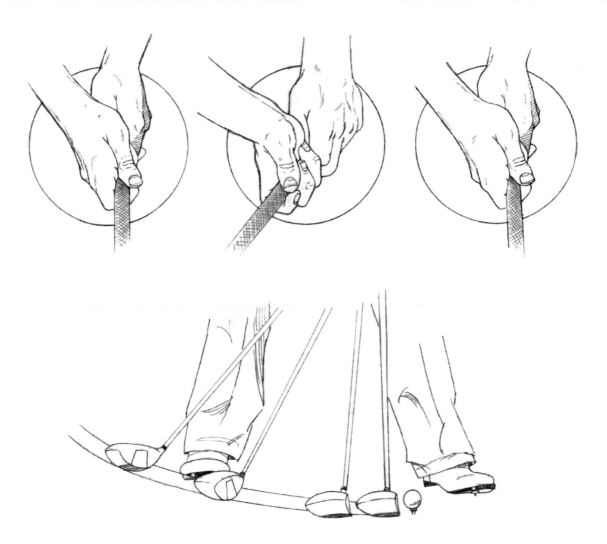

The waggle is more than a way to keep from being too static in the moments before the swing begins. An effective waggle is a preview of the rotation the hands and arms make in the backswing and the forward swing. The left hand and arm pronate, and the right hand and arm supinate going back, then reverse that order going forward.

Also, the waggle has the clubhead going back and forth on the target line in what amounts to a version of the path it will take in the swing itself at the start of the swing itself.

A RECAP OF THE BACKSWING

The backswing begins with the left shoulder turning forward, then laterally to the right. In this initial action your hands and the club may move
slightly out and away from your body. They may not. They may go
straight back for a foot or so. (Actually, there are no straight lines in a golf
swing, although it may seem that way at the very start of the swing.) But
they will not go inward or closer to your body. At this point the swing is
describing a circle.

The hands and arms remain extended until they reach about waist high.
Then the left arm rotates to the right (pronates) and the right arm bends.
The swing becomes an ellipse.

The coil of the upper body pulls the lower body into movement, a turn
to the right. The shaft of the club may get to parallel with the ground at
the top of the backswing, but even with a driver it may not. It depends on
individual flexibility and is not an issue to be concerned with. You may be
surprised to know that Lee Trevino has one of the longest swings in golf
without his club ever getting to parallel. It's because he has such a wide
radius. By retaining full radius within your particular physical framework,
you will have a long enough swing.

The Forward Swing—
a Happening

I cannot tell you what to do in the forward swing itself, because you shouldn't
consciously think of anything. I can only describe what happens and why.

The forward swing to impact, shown here with Fred Couples, features a simultaneous lateral slide and turn of the lower body to the left. The wrists remain cocked and unhinge naturally by virtue of centrifugal force. The uncocking is never made to happen. At impact, the right side is passive, and the left leg is braced to absorb the force exerted by the rest of the body.

The upper body is still coiling to the right, and the arms, hands, and club are still moving back and up when the lower body begins to go in the opposite direction—toward the target. That lower-body movement to the left eventually pulls the club down to the ball. In effect, the forward swing has two segments, but you won't notice that.

With the lateral slide of the lower left side, the left leg becomes a brace against which the rest of your body will move. Then the left hip will turn to the left. Your wrists and hands will remain cocked, or hinged. Only centrifugal force will cause the wrists to unhinge. There is never an effort to unhinge the wrists or use the right side. The entire right side is passive. This is reflected by a flexed right knee as it drives down and to the left, and by the wrists and hands remaining hinged until impact or even afterward. Ideally, if you delay the hit, as Lee Trevino does, the rotation of the upper body squares the clubface at impact and the wrists don't unhinge until after the ball is hit. Ironically, the very passivity of the right side is what produces the strongest and most accurate shot.

At impact, your right shoulder is well below the left shoulder and is working under the chin. Your left hip is past the ball and turned to the left. However, the area just above the center of your chest—the windpipe—is where it was at address.

Once past impact, your head will rotate up and to the left; all your weight is on your left leg, and at the finish your body is facing left of the target. Your right hand has rotated above the left hand, and your arms and the club have swung around your body and just above your shoulder line.

There is one basic swing idea golfers have been hearing for years and years that relates to the forward swing, which gets them into a lot of trouble; that is, keeping the head down. Of course, I don't think there should be any downswing thoughts, just as I don't think there should be any backswing thoughts other than turning the left shoulder to get started, but because "keep the head down" is so deeply entrenched in golf instruction, I feel compelled to talk about it and explain why it doesn't work.

The correct phrase should be "Keep your head in place," and that place is where your head was positioned when the swing started. Trying to keep your head down restricts the turning action of the body; it causes a stiffness in the swing and can also hurt your back. You keep your head in place to maintain your axis, your center. You have measured yourself from the ball at address based on the position of your head; therefore, if you move your head up or forward or back in the forward swing you have changed that measure and will not hit the ball in the center of the clubface.

What keeps your head in place is not actually trying to do it, but the left leg and hip moving laterally to start the forward swing. With that lateral movement, the right shoulder drops down and doesn't interfere with

Even well past impact the right shoulder remains below the left shoulder and is working under the chin. At the finish the head has rotated up and to the left, the right hand has rotated naturally to above the left hand, and the arms and club have swung around the body and just above the shoulder line.

the position of your head. It moves under your chin, so your head stays in place because nothing is forcing it out of position. If you were to start your forward swing with the upper right side or the right hip, or by throwing the club from the top with an early release of the wrist cock, that would move your spine, sternum, and head out of its center. The head moves up.

On Tempo

A lot of great players have had relatively fast swings: Ben Hogan, for instance, and Nick Price, for another. Because they have such fine co-ordination, though, they make their fast swing look easy. When working on your own swing, you should not try to achieve good tempo by starting the club back more slowly or more quickly than you naturally want to swing.

When I discuss tempo with my students, I take into consideration where they come from, the kind of work they do, and their natural rhythm. I think it is a fair generalization to say that people who come from small towns in the South or Midwest, for example, do things more slowly than people who grew up in a big city like New York or Chicago. On the same principle, a person who trades shares on the floor of the stock exchange is apt to do everything more quickly than a chemist who does a lot of careful research. Then, too, some people by their nature, no matter where they come from or what sort of work they do, have their own life tempo. You have to go with your personal flow. For instance, if the fellow from the big city who works on the stock exchange and tends to do most things quickly takes the club back too slowly, he will have to increase the speed of the club in the forward swing—jump at it, as we say—to develop enough centrifugal force commensurate with his instincts. His nature takes over when it is time to make his downswing and hit the ball. He will end up with a right-side-dominant movement, which of course is anathema to good golf.

In other words, you have to develop enough swing speed or tempo in the backswing and have it build on itself so that your instincts are satisfied that you have enough power going for you. Then your right side will leave it—and you—alone. At whatever speed you swing the club, it must be a swing. What is a swing? It is demonstrated when you whirl a rope with a weight attached to one end and develop enough centrifugal force to hold the rope extended fully and traveling on the same arc throughout. The minute you slow that rope down, it changes its length and the arc varies. The same thing happens with a golf swing.

When you are asking the big muscles of the body to create a swing plane, there has to be enough swing speed to create sufficient centrifugal force. Your left arm is the rope, and to get a plane there has to be enough swing speed to keep the left arm extended. You could have a slow swing or a fast swing, but one way or the other it has to have enough speed to develop centrifugal force. If the swing is too slow, there will be no centrifugal force and the only way to stay on plane is to force the arms to be straight. But then the arms are tense, and tense muscles don't move as fast as relaxed ones. Tension in a golf swing should develop naturally, as when you coil correctly or grip the club comfortably at address and let the pressure increase as the swing develops. The speed of a swing is an individual thing, and you have to practice and play to find the speed that is yours.

In general, though, most people try to make a slower swing, or at least start the club back slowly. This is very helpful on a number of counts. For one, golfers who start the backswing with their hands and arms rather than their shoulders avoid being too handsy in the swing if they can slow down that hands/arms movement. That's why a lot of tour pros want to start the club back slowly, so their hands won't jump the gun and get too far ahead of their upper body. The slower tempo is a Band-Aid until you learn to start the swing with the left shoulder.

Also, right-side-dominant golfers have told me that when they try to start the backswing with the left shoulder they have a problem with it because they simply don't have a lot of coordination on that side. They have to go slowly with the move to kind of nurse it into play.

Another way to smooth out the start of the swing is to stay with the thought of starting with the left shoulder a little longer into the turn.

On Weight Shifting

The proper shifting of your weight happens automatically *when you start the swing correctly*, with the turn of the left shoulder. The movement puts more weight on the right side, which is supported by the right leg. This is the definition of weight shift.

However, if the hips turn simultaneously with the upper trunk, they could counteract the shift and cause a lower-body reverse pivot. That is, the weight will remain on the left leg at the top of the backswing instead of shifting to the right. Since the upper body is connected to the club via the arms and hands, it turns in the direction the club is moving—to the right—

and should *pull* the lower body in that same direction and the right amount *when you make the proper coil*. You will then stay centered.

Another form of reverse pivot happens when the upper body tilts forward or to the left and down. This upper-body reverse pivot occurs when the right arm raises the right shoulder abruptly at the start of the backswing. Here, the right elbow usually flies out behind. This causes a sway to the right of the lower body.

The lower-body reverse pivot problem can be corrected by paying close attention to your E O L, by concentrating on starting the swing with the left shoulder, and by using the following coil or separation drills:

1. With or without a club in hand, take a good address position with your back to a wall and with your buttocks just touching the surface. Start the swing with the left shoulder and take it back until you feel a tightness or pressure in the left latissimus muscle. You will also feel more weight on your right leg. Or, without a club, simply fold your arms across your chest and make an upper-body backswing turn.

2. Stand on your right leg only and start your backswing. You don't have to make a full backswing. This drill tends to help your shoulder turn precede your lower-body turn and your weight shift.

The upper-body reverse pivot problem can be corrected with the following drill.

A. Concentrate on having your right shoulder six inches lower than your left shoulder at address, and do the left-side drills described at the end of Chapter 3. Also, make sure you start the backswing with your left shoulder.

B. Do the left-side drills.

CHAPTER THREE

Ambidexterity, the Extra Dimension

An aspect of golf instruction that has been entirely ignored so far is ambidexterity and how important it is to swinging the club well. I had already been thinking about it for some time when a conversation in the early 1970s with Dr. John Laragh, head of the hypertension department at New York Hospital, corroborated my thoughts. He had been treating Mickey Mantle and had come to realize that many superior athletes have ambidexterity. Mantle, of course, batted both ways and threw right-handed. In fact, many baseball players bat left-handed and throw right-handed, or vice versa. Ted Williams was a left-handed hitter and threw right-handed. Wade Boggs does the same thing. There are hundreds more I can name in baseball. You see it, too, in basketball players who can dribble and shoot with either hand.

In golf there are also a lot of ambidextrous players. Johnny Miller, Paul Azinger, Greg Norman, J. C. Snead, Curtis Strange, Larry Mize, and Tom Watson, among the current tour players, write left-handed and play from the right side. Both Phil Mickelson and Bob Charles, the two best left-handed golfers in the game's history, do everything else right-handed.

There are other clues to a person's ambidexterity. Right-handed player Julius Boros, for instance, used a shotgun left-handed. If so many of the best athletes have this capacity, then it must have some bearing on their talent, and for some twenty years now I have examined this thoroughly and incorporated it into my practice-tee instruction. This is the first chance I've had to detail it in writing.

Why haven't we heard anything from others about ambidexterity, from players or the notable swing gurus working with them? The main reason, I think, is that the players have ambidexterity and don't realize it. They unwittingly take it for granted and assume they are better players than the great majority because they practice and play more, have more technical information, and have a "gift." They do practice and play more than most people, do get more technical information, and do have the gift of unusual talent, but part of that gift is ambidexterity. The teaching pros who have made big reputations working with players such as Nick Faldo are credited with having special insights into the golf swing and a rare ability to communicate them to these outstanding players. Perhaps, but they are also (probably unwittingly) the beneficiaries of their players' ambidexterity.

I don't mean ambidexterity in the strictest sense: a person able to do the same things equally well both right-handed and left-handed. If that is the case, fine, but it is not necessary. What I mean is that a person who is right-side dominant—a right-hander in most things he does—will also have a high degree of coordination in his left hand or side. This is especially vital to the golf swing I teach, in which right-handed players must subjugate their right side as much as possible to the left side. This will be easier for players who have ambidexterity, because they do not instinctively rely entirely on their right side for power and control. It is not so much a matter of having a lot of strength in the opposite side, because centrifugal force built up during the swing and during the coiling and uncoiling of the left side will take care of that. Opposite-side coordination is the most important thing so the dominant side doesn't dominate the start of the swing.

What if you don't have any such ambidexterity or opposite-side coordination? I honestly think everyone has some—maybe not a lot, but some. The majority of people are right-handed, and most of them don't know they have left-side coordination because, for one thing, social mores have always discouraged left-handedness. Everyone knows cases in which young children who are natural left-handers are forced by their parents to do everything right-handed. By the same token, natural right-handers are not encouraged to do anything left-handed, and in effect they let any left-handedness they do have atrophy by not using it. For example, they could very well comb their hair with their left hand; turn the knob of a door to open it with their left hand, or use the key left-handed; cut their food with the right hand and take it to their mouth with the fork in their left hand, instead of switching to the right hand. These are little things that seem inconsequential, but they would increase coordination with the left hand, and a consciousness of the left side, both of which are good for playing golf right-handed. As it happens, natural left-handers who are well coordinated with their right side and *play golf right-handed* have an advantage over everyone else. But natural right-handers can do something about this.

There is no question that a dominant right hand can be a great disadvantage in some sports. I think this is one reason that the two-handed set shot went out of basketball. The right hand would too often overpower the left, causing the ball to be thrown off line. It may be that no one really knew the right hand was the culprit in the two-handed set shot—perhaps it was an instinctive response—but in any case the one-handed shot took over because it eliminated the problem. In golf, cross-handed putting helps solve the dominant right-hand problem. By extending the left hand lower down on the handle of the club, it becomes dominant and the right hand becomes passive.

But even if you have no opposite-side coordination at all, *you can obtain ambidexterity in your golf game by doing the things I teach in the setup and during the swing.* (Again, in all the above and what follows, left-handers need only switch the reference to their right hand/right side.) I also have some off-course drills for obtaining ambidexterity, outlined later in this chapter. What follows are repeat descriptions of the main elements of my system, but this time I want to point out how each serves to enhance left-sidedness, which is absolutely vital to playing your best golf. The right side must in all respects be subjugated, made as subordinate to the left side as possible. That is a central premise.

Let's start with the grip. If you set the club in the crook of the left index finger and under the heel pad of the left hand and hold the handle with the last three fingers of the hand, you activate the muscle that runs up to the top of your left forearm. This gives your left arm and hand a degree of strength it may not actually have, keeps the left arm firm throughout the swing, and makes it dominant over the right hand and side. I am not implying, however, that you try to hold the club any more firmly with the left hand than with the right, just differently. This allows you to hold the club with the hand as well as the fingers.

Furthermore, when the club is held correctly in the left hand, the left thumb does not extend down the handle—it shortens up a little. This reinforces the hold on the club at the top of the swing—the club won't flop around, because the thumb is supporting it. Also, the right hand fits around the left thumb more comfortably in its shortened state and doesn't have the urge to become more active. Finally, by having only the right side of the right thumb touching the handle, the right hand is less prone to be active.

Now, how does the right shoulder, being six inches lower than the left shoulder at address, produce ambidexterity? Because all the muscles on the right side of your body, especially in the pectoral and armpit areas and in the back, are slack and relaxed. This allows the left-side back muscles to contract during the backswing and produce a good coil. If the right shoulder is higher than the left, or even level, there is a right-side tension that takes over the swing.

Take that a step further. At address, right-side-dominant people would do well not to hyperextend their right arm—lock the elbow. Let that arm be no straighter than when it is hanging easily at your side. In fact, a lot of older tour players, from an era when golf didn't have the more athletic—and ambidextrous—players it now has, used to crimp their right arm at address. This exaggeration of the soft right arm subjugated their right side. Arnold Palmer, Bobby Toski, Charlie Sifford, Miller Barber, and many other tour pros do this. I think it is an excellent thing for right-side-dominant players to do.

Next let's look at the address. If you stand too far from the ball at address, the right side will overextend and become dominant, because the club will be pulled in toward you at the start of the backswing. Then, you can't get your left side properly coiled before your hands reach the top of the backswing, and you will unhinge the hands too soon in the forward swing. National long-drive champion Art Sellinger used an expression about the swing plane I teach that is appropriate here. He said it was like Little Red Riding Hood taking the long way to Grandma's house. In other words, by having your hands stay the same distance, or increase their distance from your body as the backswing begins, it takes the hands longer to get to the top. This gives you time to coil the upper body completely and let the lower body move forward first.

If you are aimed to the right of your target at address, you will have to use your right side to whip the club inside too quickly in the backswing. You'll then have to raise it and in the forward swing come over the top—push your right shoulder forward toward the ball—to get the clubhead going down the target line at impact. This invites a right-side takeover. You'll never have ambidexterity by aiming to the right of your target, which is the most common aiming mistake.

By keeping your feet apart the width of your shoulders (from the insoles) with your driver, you get more lower-body resistance to turning. Also, by starting the swing with the turn of the left shoulder, you resist lateral movement and can really load up your upper left side with your coil and extend the club more. This will help you be more left-sided in the forward swing.

The waggle I recommend, with the arms and hands supinating and pronating so the clubface goes from square to open to square, is a left-side maneuver.

So what about the Four Fundamentals, and how do they relate to ambidexterity?

Basically, you want the left side to dominate the backswing because the left arm will stay out and away from your body. You will get full radius and have time to coil. If you let your right arm dominate, a consistent arc is unlikely, because the right elbow folds and changes length.

Earlier I mentioned that in creating a good radius, the hands at the beginning of the swing stay the same distance from your body as at address or increase that distance—move farther from the body. If you have a lot of genetic ambidexterity, your hands will almost invariably move farther from your body in the first stages of the backswing. I mention this to make you aware that it shouldn't be regarded as something wrong. At the same time, you should not *try* to do it.

How does being open at address promote left-side dominance? It puts the upper left side of the body in a position where it has the urge to start and a place to go. Because the hips are also open, when you start the upper body before the lower body you create a lot of torque or coil in the left side of the back early in the swing. This torque is essential to making a good coil. You don't generate much power in any sport without torque.

The left-side coil is the power that makes you ambidextrous. By rotating to the right, the big muscles on the left side, which are attached to the left hip and pelvic girdle, are activated. This loading up of the left side makes it dominant and subjugates the right side. You will find this especially valuable on pitch shots in the fifty- to seventy-yard range, because your feet and hips are open even more than usual. You can be fully wound up before your hands reach your armpits. It will be almost impossible to go over the top (throw your right shoulder out toward the ball) in the forward swing, or spin out (turn the right hip sharply left with no weight transfer to the left).

Erectness—having proper posture at address—affects ambidexterity because it allows you to rotate your upper body within the area it starts in. This gets the chest out of the way of the upper part of the left arm. The left arm can extend fully. If you are not properly erect, your chest won't turn as well. It will be in the way of your left arm, which will have to bend and weaken your radius. Good upper-body rotation allows you to stretch your left latissimus.

Good body posture allows you freedom to rotate your body. When the main spine is bent over too much, the head is down too low. This blocks the freedom of the shoulder turn. Left-sidedness is lost, because a full coil becomes difficult.

Centering is significantly related to ambidexterity, because rotating within the space of your body immediately puts a good stretch on the left latissimus. If you sway, you will eventually turn but won't coil early. *This gives the hands a chance to reach the top of the backswing and get prepared to hit before the coil is complete.*

Of course, by starting the swing with a turn of the left shoulder, all the other left-side-oriented actions described above will occur. It is the most obvious left-sided action of all. However, I prefer to talk about it here not in terms of mechanics, but as a mental routine.

Mechanical Mindset vs. Athletic Mindset

Let me say right off that *the mere thought* of starting the golf swing with the left shoulder turn makes you ambidextrous; makes you left-sided. If you don't have a left-side thought, or key, to begin the swing, the right side will dominate the action. Why? Because, if you are right-handed, *no left-side thought means right-side dominance.* Activating the left side subjugates the right side. A right-sided person who thinks left-sided becomes a left-hander, or at least a partial left-hander. Otherwise, there is no logical reason for the right-handed person not to let that side dominate his golf swing, especially under the pressure of a crucial shot. If the right-dominant person has no left-sided thought in the moment before he starts the swing, or no thought at all, his right side will dominate because it requires no thought for it to do so—it is natural instinct. People tell me that I personally don't have to think about left-sidedness anymore, because I've been doing it for so long. Not so. There hasn't been a shot I've played for close to thirty years when I haven't thought of my left side, because I know that the minute I don't think about it I'll go right back to being a right-hander. A natural right-hander is not going to take the club back with the right side, then have the left side take over on the forward swing. That is just not going to happen. Once the right side gets into the act, it is in to stay. A right-side backswing means a right-side forward swing, and that means hitting the ball without the delay of the right side.

In a way, this idea of *thinking* left-sided is more important than the actual address positions—grip, stance, and so forth. You can be in the right position at address and still be right-sided in the swing if you don't think about the left-side move. Which brings me to the point of *when* to think of the left-shoulder move. It should come an instant before the swing begins. *And not only should it be your very last thought before going into action, it should be preceded by no thought at all.*

I am speaking on the assumption that you have learned the mechanics of the setup and the various preswing techniques I have outlined here so that you do them more or less by second nature. You have moved up beside the ball and taken your address position. You continue to move your feet and are waggling the club. At this point you are not thinking of anything; you are like the engine of a car that has been turned on but the driver has not yet shifted into gear. Because motion plus no thought puts you in an athletic mode, you are eager to start. When you think of starting the swing with the left shoulder, that is when you get into gear and actually start the swing.

Why do it this way? When you start the swing with the left shoulder, every muscle in your body is going to move as a result, within a second and in the correct order. Your brain knows all these things are going to move, but if it has to direct them, to *tell* them what to do, it is going to be overloaded. If you have such thoughts as "Am I open enough?" "Is my grip right?" "Am I aiming right?" the brain can't get all those body parts ready to go. Consequently, the body parts don't react well. You don't get a good coil or a fluid backswing. You're in stutter state, as I call it, because you have overloaded the brain. You freeze, lose natural momentum, lose athleticism. You suffer paralysis by analysis, as Ernest Jones put it many years ago. The brain needs a few seconds to get everything ready for the wake-up call, which is the start with the left shoulder. That way you have momentum, for which I have a formula: *Momentum equals motion plus no thought.*

You can stand over the ball for a whole minute and still have momentum, and you can stand over it for only a couple of seconds and not have good momentum because you have thoughts. We are all familiar with how long Jack Nicklaus stands over a shot, especially a putt, before drawing the club back. *What he is doing is draining his mind of all thought before beginning the action.* That is what you must do. Some people may take longer than others to get drained, but so be it. There is no prescribed time that everyone must adhere to. To put a time frame on it would defeat the concept.

When you set up to hit a golf shot, you cannot do it mechanically and do it really well time after time. There are too many integrated factors involved—getting the right distance from the ball, having the right posture, width of stance, weight distribution. If you think of each of those things when preparing to play a shot, it is like walking on hot coals. You will do one, then stop, do another, then stop, and so on. Your body will inevitably tighten up to such an extent that, for one thing, you won't achieve those positions entirely—your right shoulder may not get down low enough in relation to the left shoulder. And you won't move into the shot with an easy flow, with momentum.

I am not saying you never do the mechanical portion of setting up consciously. Just as in any other education process, you must learn the details. But you practice them at home or perhaps in your office, not when actually hitting shots—not even practice shots. You will probably work on the details of the setup on the practice tee, but even here I advise my students to step off to the side to go through them. When hitting the ball, even in practice, you have to trust that you will have the positions right. You are better off half or three-quarters correct at the ball and not thinking about anything (except the left-shoulder move), because you will make a freer swing. A free-flowing swing from an incorrect position will be better than a stiff one from a good position. You want your body *to know it is getting ready to start a golf swing.* That knowing comes from being beside the ball, waggling the club, and moving your feet up and down in place, *not* from thinking about all the different positions you should be in.

MOTIVATION, MOMENTUM, THE FIRST MOVE

Here is the three-step process for making every golf shot:

Motivation: You have to have a target in mind before you walk up to the ball. Glance at it and *burn it into your mind*. That is your motivation. Without it, you will not be inspired to play. You are not a robot; you are not made of steel. There is nothing to make you swing the club except the motivation to reach a target with the ball. Theoretically, you could get the club to the top of the backswing with a nice coil, good center, lots of radius, right on plane, and just walk away if you didn't have the motivation to unload and make the forward swing.

Motivation begins before you move up to the ball. Once you have it, you don't have to worry about aiming. As I remarked in Chapter One, you are like the third baseman who goes to his left for a grounder and when he gets the ball just wheels toward first and throws; he doesn't have to look toward first base; he *knows* where it is. The same with you and your golf target.

Momentum: Now you go through your setup routine with a flowing motion, all the parts falling into place. You are not thinking of anything consciously. You are waggling and moving your feet in place. Your inner clock will tell you when you are ready to swing. You will take just about the same amount of time every time. If you try to regulate yourself with a certain number of waggles, let's say, or decide to walk up to the ball and hit it quickly to overcome tension, you are doing something arbitrarily and being mechanical; you will be out of sync, and won't have good momentum.

The First Move: Without thought, you will *feel itchy* to go, to start the swing. Think of the move of the left shoulder, and go.

Left vs. Right

It is important to have a complete understanding of ambidexterity and its impact on your golf; to study how right-side dominance violates the four fundamentals of my system: Center, Radius, Plane, and Coil.

CENTER

There are four ways to lose your center with an overdominant right side.

1. The most common is the **reverse pivot**. That is, your upper body moves to the left during the backswing and in the opposite direction during the forward swing. It is a reverse pivot because the body should be moving to the right on the backswing and to the left on the forward swing. A reverse pivot often includes not only the shifting error but also a tilting of the body with the right side rising too quickly at the start of the swing. The spine tilts forward, and you have come out of your center.

You can check yourself on this by swinging a golf club with only your left hand/arm. If there is no left side forward tilt, you'll know the right side has been too dominant in your regular swing action.

Why do people lift the right side at the start of the swing?

a. The right shoulder is not low enough at address to allow the muscles on the right side to be relaxed. Sometimes the right-side dominance is so great that the right shoulder is actually higher than the left. We have all seen golfers stand at the ball that way and have rarely seen them hit a good shot.

b. The club is not held correctly in the right hand; it is more in the palm than in the fingers, which also leads to tension in the right arm. The right arm dominates the start of the backswing and hikes up the right shoulder so abruptly that it tilts your body to the left.

c. The position of the right hand is either too strong or weak in relation to how it hangs naturally at your side (see Chapter One). If the right hand is too high or weak—twisted too far to the left—the muscles in the arm are tensed. Out of that tension comes overdominance, because the tension creates a demand to be eased. As a result, the backswing tends to be jerky at the start, and this in turn pulls the body out of its axis.

The right hand may be twisted too much to the right—in a strong position. This is also very common among right-side-dominant golfers. The position encourages bringing the right arm in toward the body at the start of the backswing. It can also hike the body up out of its center.

2. The **upper-body sway** to the right to start the backswing is another common cause of losing your axis. In this case, the dominant right side pulls the body laterally to the right. This derives from the natural instinct to rear back and throw an object. In golf, the trigger for this pulling to the right is a right-hand grip that is either too weak or too strong. It may also come from the right shoulder not being lower than the left at address. From this dominant right-sided setup, the right shoulder and hand/arm are too fired up before the swing even starts; and when it does get under way, the right-side muscles fire too much and overpower the left side in the takeaway.

When you have moved out of your center in this way, you have essentially lost your balance. This imbalance denies you the ability to spring forward with your weight in the forward swing. You now have to push your right side to the left, which moves your head, sternum, and windpipe ahead of the ball. The upper body is ahead of the ball at impact, causing a great loss of power and very often an inaccurate shot, usually a push off-line to the right. A good analogy to this is found in baseball. There has never been a home-run hitter who leaned well back to the right with his weight on his right side as he stood in the batter's box. All home-run hitters stand with their weight equally distributed, then step forward with the left foot to start the swing at the ball. With that step of the left foot their weight is on their right foot, but they haven't leaned their body in that direction. Their weight is to the right, but they remain in balance. The center is held, just as it must be for golfers.

3. Many golfers **lose the center forward** toward the ball when they either lock the right knee or straighten it in the backswing, rather than keep it slightly flexed. This usually occurs when the right hip gets too active in the takeaway. The result is a forward tilt, with the left shoulder dropping forward toward the ball. The corresponding move in the forward swing will have the left shoulder raising up and moving backward. This is a very ineffective way to swing the club and with irons cause a shank—hitting the ball where the shaft and clubhead are joined.

4. Sometimes the **center is lost backward** by pulling away from the ball at the start of the swing. This move is often in conjunction with the lifting up of the body—the upper body moving farther away from the ball than it was at address. When this happens, the upper body must move toward the ball in the forward swing; too often, the move is too far forward. When you lose your axis in this way, a lot of shots are hit near the heel of the club with the woods or metals, or with irons in the shank.

This action is the result of the same right-hand grip problem that caused the sway—it's too strong or too weak—and a fired-up right side at address that explodes or overpowers the left in the takeaway. In this case, the left shoulder actually goes slightly up as it turns; sometimes the head also raises.

5. A **lower-body reverse pivot** is caused by inability to start the upper left side of the body moving (turning) before the lower body. This happens when tension is created in the right arm and hand that prevents the upper left side from starting the backswing. The player substitutes lower-body movement, but the hips turn too much and the weight stays too much on the left leg.

Another scenario would be the right leg straightening and moving backward and to the left as the swing begins. This can be avoided by starting the swing with the left shoulder before the legs and hips turn. The weight is immediately thrown to the right leg, and it becomes the post to turn on.

RADIUS

The left arm is the radius of the swing, and it should stay at its normal length. Right-sided mistakes that occur and prevent the left arm from staying at its normal length are:

- The right hand and arm pull the left arm into the body, bending the left arm.
- An abrupt lifting of the right shoulder and arm at the start of the takeaway causes the left arm to be blocked by the left side of

the chest, which doesn't have enough time to turn and get out of the way. The left arm has to bend.

- By bending the right arm early and far more than it was bent at address, the left arm is also bent.

- Pulling the upper torso sideways into a sway can cause the left arm to be lodged behind the chest and to bend to get around it.

- The right hand is so dominant that the right palm is pulled away from the thumb of the left hand. This, too, can cause the left arm to bend.

PLANE

There are two violations of the plane that occur from right-side dominance; you either go over or under your correct plane. I am only going to deal with the backswing plane because, as I have said elsewhere, if the backswing is okay, the forward swing will be okay.

1. Swinging **under the plane**, or too flat, results when the right arm and hand pull the club to the inside—closer to the body—at the very start of the backswing. This causes too flat an arc. The culprit is a grip in which the right hand is too far under the handle.

2. Swinging **above the plane** is a right-shoulder problem that imitates the action of chopping wood. The golf club gets too vertical, too quickly, after the start of the backswing. As a result, the right arm raises vertically without supinating (rotating around its own axis). Very often, the right elbow "flies"—juts out behind.

The arms must rotate in essentially the same way that the body does as the swing progresses from the takeaway. The supination of the right arm and the corresponding pronation of the left arm are what puts the club on the correct plane.

COIL

When the *upper body* turns or rotates as much as possible and far more than the lower body, you have a proper, full coil. But this must be in conjunction with a relatively stable lower body at the start of the swing, thereby creating a positive tension for the downswing.

An overactive lower body is almost always the result of right-side dominance and prevents the upper body from beginning to turn before the lower body. You can also lose your coil with a right-side-dominant move in which the right shoulder becomes very active and pulls the left shoulder too horizontally. A right arm and hand that overpower the left arm and hand in the takeaway can pull, lift, or lower the upper trunk out of position so it cannot turn before the lower body does. Improper grip and setup positions activate these overpowering moves of the right arm and hand, which are either too much under or on top of the club, and/or in the palm. The right arm may also be too stiff at address, or the right shoulder too high. In other words, the right hand and arm are loaded for bear!

Drills to Develop Ambidexterity

Here are five drills I give my students, and use myself, to enhance left-sidedness:

1. Take an iron, preferably a middle or short iron, and with only the left hand hold it upside down by the hosel. Swing it back and through.

The club will feel very light. This will give you a good sense of how the swing should feel, how the left arm puts the club on plane and creates a radius. Think of turning the left shoulder to start the drill.

One of the drills (#1) to develop greater left-sidedness is to hold a short or middle iron upside down with only the left hand, which is on the hosel. Swing it back and through with a turning of the left shoulder, keeping the right arm behind your back to make the body turn more easily.

2. Again with a middle or short iron, hold it right-side up about six inches off the ground and with only the left hand. Swing the iron back with a turn of the left shoulder, then let it swing through. It is a good way to get the sense of swinging on the correct plane. This exercise will let you feel how the left side works. The correct turn of the left shoulder is essential to this exercise. For the above two exercises, I recommend putting your right arm behind your back, because it is easier to turn.

Another version (#2) of the previous ambidexterity drill, in which you swing the club with only the left hand and arm. This time hold the middle or short iron right-side up, but hold it a few inches off the ground. Swing it back, starting with a turn of the left shoulder, then swing it through. Along with enhancing left-sidedness, this drill will give you a feel for swinging on the correct plane, and how the left side works.

3. Take your standard grip, then open your right hand and hold the palm against the left thumb. Swing the club back and through, keeping the palm of the right hand on the club and open. Don't hit balls. This drill will give you the feeling of the right side being pulled down and through the ball, but most important, it will give you the feel of the left-side takeaway.

In this ambidexterity enhancement drill (#3), take your standard grip on the club, then open your right hand and hold only the palm against the left thumb. Swing the club back and through, keeping the right hand on the club and open in this way. Don't hit balls, just absorb the feeling of the left-side takeaway and the right side being pulled down through the impact zone.

4. Make a fist with your right hand and lay it against the side of the handle. Keep it in place and swing the club back and through.

The Catch-It Drill (#5) to enhance ambidexterity begins with your right hand off the club and open and positioned about shoulder width to the side and a bit forward of your left hand and the club. Start your swing with the turn of the left shoulder. When the club reaches your right hand, hold it against the club and complete the swing. This drill also helps build extension in the backswing.

5. Hold your right hand open about two feet directly to the right or behind and a bit forward of your left hand and the club. Start your swing with the turn of the left shoulder, and when the club reaches the right hand, take hold of it and complete your swing. I call this the Catch-It Drill. It helps increase extension in the swing.

6. Put the palm of your right hand underneath your left elbow so it supports the bony part of the elbow with the fingers wrapped around the outside of the arm. In effect, you have put your right arm between your left arm and your body. Now make a turn as if you were starting your backswing. You will find there is no way your left arm can move closer to your body at the start of your swing. That's the point of the drill—to give you a sense of extending your radius, not sucking it in.

All the drills outlined here are designed to enhance your sense of how the left side feels in starting the swing. You should find time to do a few exercises before hitting each ball on the course. You can even do them in the house, or in your office when you get a free moment. It is especially worthwhile doing them when, during a round, you feel the wheels coming off your game. A few exercises can help you get back on your stick.

CHAPTER FOUR

Shaping Shots and the Short Game

One of the great pleasures of golf is to make the ball curve in flight or go lower or higher than normal. It is fun to do in itself and also helps keep your basic swing healthy. But it is also necessary. A tree or group of trees or some other obstruction in the direct line to the target is mainly why every golfer needs the ability to shape shots. That's obvious, but what many golfers don't understand about shaping golf shots is that it should be done without altering your basic swing pattern. And it can be done.

It really doesn't take a lot of manipulation to get a ball to turn from right to left or from left to right or to go lower or higher than usual. The key to any of these shots is in the setup to the ball. After that you make the same initial move to start the swing—the turn of the left shoulder. That may be the single most important thing to know about shot shaping. By not altering your basic swing you will make solid contact with the ball, and that is as vital to shaping shots as it is for standard, straight-away ones.

Hitting Draws and Fades

A **draw** is what you might call a miniature hook, the ball curving right to left anywhere from one to four yards. A ball curving more than that is a hook. The technique for each is essentially the same, with the hook simply requiring a little more of it. But there is something else that helps to make these shots come off that has nothing to do with mechanics, and that is visualization. By picturing in your mind the shape of the shot you intend to hit, you have an excellent chance of pulling it off.

In terms of technique alone, the right-to-left shot is accomplished mainly with an alteration of the grip. The left hand is made stronger—that is, it is twisted a little more to the right than normally. As a basic guideline, the **V** formed by the left thumb and forefinger is on a line *to the right* of your right shoulder. Let me emphasize, however, that is *only a guideline*. Where the **V** actually aims for a draw or hook depends on where your **V** is pointed in your standard grip. For the draw, the twist of the left hand will simply not be as much as for the hook.

The right hand changes by rearranging the right index finger. The crook in which the club is set moves to the bottom, or under the handle. The **V** formed by the index finger and thumb will point approximately to the right shoulder or just to the right of it.

Aim at a secondary target to the right of your actual target. The secondary target is determined from your experience with how much draw or hook you get when you try for these shots. At impact, stay back on your right side just a bit and roll your hands over to the left.

But before the mechanics, picture the shape of the shot in your mind.

And if your natural shot is a fade, picture the draw or hook even more vividly—*and many times* before getting up to play the shot.

The **fade** is when the ball moves in the air from left to right from one to four yards. A slice is when the ball moves a lot more in that direction. For these shots, reverse the grip adjustment used for the draw and hook. The left hand is weakened slightly; it is twisted a bit more than normal to the left. The V is pointed toward the left shoulder. Again, reposition the right hand, changing only the index finger of the right hand. For the left-to-right shot it is set so the crook is along the side of the handle and near the top of it. The V on this hand is pointed approximately toward the center of your chest.

Naturally, your aim for the fade is to the left of the real target, in this case with your stance open—your right foot in front of your left or closer to the ball. Pick out a tree or some other object and make that your secondary target. The setup of your body—the alignment of your feet, your hips, and shoulders—is oriented toward it. How much should you allow for the curve of the ball? Again, that is a matter of personal judgment based on experience. Practice these shots to find out how much curve you get, and take that experience with you onto the golf course. Keep in mind, too, that the ball will react differently under less than perfect conditions. For instance, it is harder to make a ball curve in any direction when playing out of wet grass—moisture reduces the amount of spin that can be put on a golf ball.

There is another, somewhat more subtle way to alter your grip for draws and fades without actually doing it on the handle itself. Take your standard grip on the club. For the draw lay the clubface a little closed behind the ball at address. Now square the clubface by rolling it to the right a little (opening it). The act of opening the blade will put your hands in the same strong, hooking position you get by actually changing the position of your hands.

For the fade take your normal grip with the face a little open, then at address turn the clubface slightly closed. In either case, you make your standard swing at the ball. The grip alone will help cause the ball to fly right-to-left or left-to-right.

Preswing visualization of these shots will get your body to do what it should in the swing. For the draw, your weight will stay back a bit longer during the forward swing, and as a result your arms and hands will roll over counterclockwise a bit more quickly. You will stay behind the ball a little longer. For the fade, you will turn your left side a little more quickly because of your open stance, and after impact pull the club to the inside along with your body and foot line at address. You will hold back the release of the hands a little. But you must not consciously think of doing those things, because you will overdo them. Infuse your mind with the visualization of the shot and then let it happen. Trust your athletic instincts. You have them. Everyone does.

Hitting the ball higher or lower than usual takes only a small adjustment in ball placement. For the **low ball**, set up with the ball a little more to the right of where you would ordinarily play it. For the **high ball**, set it up a little more toward your left foot.

There is not much more to these shots, except under extreme circumstances. If the ball must be hit exceptionally low, play it back a bit farther in your stance and hood the blade a little (close it) or it will be aiming to the right. I also recommend using a club with less loft than the distance might require, and choking down on the handle a little. Make a lateral slide of the hips to the left early in the downswing.

To get a ball even higher, such as over a tall tree that is fairly near to you, play the ball more toward your left foot. You might also open the face of the club a little. If you do, aim a bit more to the left to accommodate the slight left-to-right flight the face position will bring. At impact, hang back—keep some weight on the right side a little longer at impact.

Here again, for both these shots the swing itself does not change from your basic action, which begins with the turning of the left shoulder. Visualization of the shots will go a long way toward directing your body to do the things it must to provide the mechanics.

Playing from Unlevel Lies— the Sidehillers

The main reason golfers have trouble playing from unlevel lies, especially when the ball is above or below the feet, is that they do not stand the correct distance from the ball and have poor posture. Both these problems, as I suggested earlier, are eliminated when you use my system for getting into the address position. The process begins with your first step up to the ball. With your right foot forward, set the clubhead down with its toe about two inches from the ball. The butt of the club is very close to your pelvis. Step back a little and open up your body—half face the target— then take a short step with the right foot. Your weight should be on your right foot from heel to ball. Your knees are under your hips. Your hips are under your midsection and only your shoulders are tilted. Again, the butt

Sidehill, Ball Above and Below Feet. By getting into the stance in exactly the same way as for standard level lie shots, you will be the correct distance from the ball and have proper erectness. Your basic swing will not change. The only adjustment you make is in aiming. With the ball above your feet, aim a few yards right of your target to allow for the right-to-left trajectory that almost invariably results. With the ball below your feet, aim a few yards to the left of your actual target, because shots off this type of lie usually move from left to right. In either case, the deviation from the normal flight pattern will be less than you think because the setup at the ball will help you make solid contact with it. The same posture is used for all these shots, which is facilitated by the routine for setting up to the ball described in Chapter One.

of the club is close to your pelvis. Then position your left foot and pull your right foot back even with it. Bend about 20 degrees at the waist, get a bit of flex in your knees, and you are ready to go. You will be the correct distance from the ball and have proper erectness. Make your standard swing, beginning with a turn of the left shoulder.

However, there are some special adjustments in regard to aiming. With *the ball below your feet*, aim a few yards left of your actual target because the ball tends to slide to the right in flight off these lies. For *a ball above your feet*, aim a few yards to the right because the shots tend to move in the air from right to left. You will find that the allowances for the curve of the ball in flight will be much less than you have probably been making, because you will be making more solid contact with the ball by being the correct distance from it at address. You will also have the same posture with all clubs and for all types of lies—a great advantage.

UPHILL AND DOWNHILL LIES

On **uphill lies** most instruction advises golfers to play the ball more forward in their stance. I say no. I think ball placement should be where it is for normal shots; if anything, the ball should be played back a tad more than usual. The reason being, it is harder to transfer your weight to the left in the forward swing when it has to go uphill. The more you play the ball forward, the less chance you have of getting your weight to the left. You are apt to hit the ball too far left of your target.

On **downhill lies**, though, I recommend playing the ball back a bit more than normal so the downswing path of the clubhead matches the slope of the ground and you catch the ball, not the ground behind it.

Uphill and Downhill Lies. On uphill lies I advise playing the ball as you would normally, not farther forward in the stance as most instruction says. With the ball more forward, the weight shift to the left must be exaggerated, and you are less likely to hit a solid and accurate shot.

However, for downhill lies the ball position should vary from normal; in this case, align the ball a bit farther back in your stance so the club has a better, steeper angle of descent that gets the ball properly airborne.

Also, depending on the severity of the slope, you will hit the ball higher or lower than standard—higher going uphill, lower going downhill. You will have to take more or less club, respectively, than the actual distance calls for.

Otherwise, get into your address position in the prescribed way and make your regular swing.

The Bunker Shot

I have come to the conclusion that for the green-side bunker shot (the explosion in the 30-yard and shorter range), not everyone has to swing the club back to the outside with an exaggerated upcocking of the wrists. That has been the conventional teaching for many years, but my own experience and my observation of the game's best bunker players have led me to believe that the swing for the explosion shot may or may not be the basic swing. There is an adjustment for one type of swing, but for the most part by being consistent to your normal swing path you reduce the risk of mis-hitting these shots.

First of all, the backswing for explosion shots must be upright or vertical and it must get that way very soon in the backswing because the overall swing is relatively short in length; it is little more than a half swing. Second, in order to play well out of bunkers you have to know what kind of swing in general you make. I'll use examples of noted players I have discussed this shot with. Gary Player takes the club back to the inside in his basic golf swing without breaking his wrists early. But that swing won't work in the bunker, because the hands and the club stay fairly low until late in the swing; the club does not get vertical soon enough. So what Gary Player—and anyone who has his type of back-swing—has to do is cock his wrists very quickly at the start of his back-swing in order to get the club vertical. At the same time, he must firm his left arm because an early wrist cock tends to soften the left arm. This early cocking of the wrists amounts to altering the swing path—the club goes back straighter or less inside—but that change occurs *without a conscious effort.* The central *feeling* is that the swing path is the same as always. There are other ways of adapting an inside-takeaway swing to the explosion shot. Having more weight on your left leg at address helps get the club go up more quickly. Chi-Chi Rodriguez does this. Chi-Chi also puts his right hand very high on the handle, in a very weak position, which also gets the club started to the outside in the backswing.

Now, Lee Trevino playing out of a bunker has to make no alterations at all from his normal swing because he does not let his hands get closer to his body at the start of his backswing—in his case they go a little far-ther away from his body. His move raises the arms and hands quickly enough for the explosion shot. The next time you watch him play that shot you will see that he does not cock his wrists dramatically in the take-away. In effect then, the kind of swing I teach is ideally suited for the bunker shot. If your hands go straight back or away from your body at the start of your backswing, you just go with that in the bunker.

But if you are using your basic swing, whatever it may be, why should you stand with your feet open for the explosion shot? You do this because the swing is going to be much shorter than a full swing, and therefore you do not activate the big muscles of your trunk the way you ordinarily would. By opening your feet at address—a line across the toes would be about 45 degrees to the left of your target—you will get an early and full coiling motion. To get the proper direction on the shot, you compensate for the open stance and the swing path from outside to inside the target line by laying the clubface open proportionate to the openness of the feet and swing path. The clubface then comes through and directs the ball to the target.

On level lies, visualize hitting about two inches behind the ball. For downhill lies you do need a more vertical swing path than normal, and you have to hit three or four inches behind the ball. In this circumstance play the ball back a bit farther in your stance.

As for distance, I put the shot into categories. For explosions of up to ten yards, the line of your feet is well open at address, about 45 degrees, and the blade is open accordingly. For shots from ten to twenty yards, your feet and the clubface are still some 45 degrees open, but you make a slightly bigger swing. From twenty to thirty yards, though, the stance and clubface are less open. For explosions of thirty to forty yards, the stance is only 5 degrees open, and the clubface is squared or slightly open. In general, the longer the explosion the less open the stance and clubface and the farther back in your stance you play the ball. I give you degrees of openness for this shot, but they are only parameters. You have to experiment to find what is right for you.

However, distance for these shots is not just a matter of stance and clubface. Just as for the pitch shot, chip shot, and putt, distance from the sand is controlled by your hands. The swing itself is a blend of arms swinging and wrists upcocking. The club goes almost straight up. The size of the swing determines how far the ball will go, and it is the hands that sense, feel, and judge how big the swing should and will be.

People ask me why the left shoulder isn't the key element in this, just as it is for so much else in my system. It is, and it isn't. Physiologically, the hands have more nerve ends that are closer to the surface of the skin than in the left shoulder, so they are essential to the touch needed for these delicate shots. What's more, for explosion shots up to thirty yards long you don't want any extension of the arms in the backswing; the backswing must be virtually vertical. Using the left shoulder creates extension. However, for explosions of more than thirty yards I recommend a less-open stance and a fuller backswing.

As for lower-body movement on the backswing; it exists only in relation to how much upper-body turn there is in the swing. For the shortest explosions there will be practically no lower-body movement; for the longer explosions, a little.

The distance you'll get when exploding out of a bunker is also affected by the type of sand from which you are playing. If the sand is soft, you must open the blade more so the club can slide under and through more easily. This type of sand puts up a lot of resistance to the clubhead.

From sand that is packed tightly (sometimes because it is wet), the face is not as open at address. It might be a good idea to use a pitching wedge or even a nine-iron, as these clubs have a sharper leading edge than the sand wedge and will cut through the sand more readily. This is a particularly good idea for the longer explosions, regardless of the texture of the sand.

In all these shots, however, you try to hit behind the ball about the same amount—a couple of inches on level lies, four inches or so when the lie is downhill.

For the **fairway bunker** shot, when you are making a full swing usually with a long club—a four-iron, say—the conventional wisdom is to make sure you catch the ball first. That often leads to catching it thin, hitting the ball somewhere up on the cover rather than at the bottom. Yes, you do want to catch the ball first, but my feeling is that it is more important to make sure you get the ball out of the bunker. If you hit it thin, it is liable to catch the lip and stay in the sand. For that reason, I recommend making sure you hit into the sand. To that end, with my practice swing outside the bunker I make sure the club hits the ground so I have the feel of doing that when in the sand. Even if I hit a touch behind the ball, I know it will get out.

Otherwise, for the fairway bunker shot go through the same setup procedure as for all other full-swing shots, with the shoulders and hips open. However, I do recommend choking down a little on the grip to accommodate the depth your feet are sunk into the sand (actually below it).

Pitching and Chipping

For pitch shots in the thirty- to sixty-yard range, and for chipping, take a good look at the illustration on page 116 of Tommy Bolt. He is hitting a chip shot, but his position at the ball is also the one I think is best for the pitch shot. *His hands are very close to his body, and his hips are straight up and under his midsection.* Notice that there is no significant bend at the waist. This is not the so-called athletic position used for regular full-swing shots that features the buttocks thrust out behind. The closeness of the hands to the body at address is important to both of these shots. I have noticed that all good pitchers and chippers take this tight position. You want your hands close to your body so the club swings back in a relatively straight line. If your hands are too far from your body, you will swing the club around yourself too much. The swing path for these shots must be tighter, more controlled; swinging straight back and straight through accomplishes this.

Pitching and Chipping. This illustration is of Tommy Bolt, who, I feel, best illustrates the correct setup for short pitches and for chip shots. The hands are very close to his body, the hips are straight up and under his midsection, and there is very little bend at the waist. All of this enhances a tighter, more controlled short swing and solid ball contact.

Otherwise, at address the feet are open 20 to 35 degrees in relation to the parallel line. For the pitch shot in particular, this allows you to create torque or body coil early in the backswing. The feet are kept fairly close together, although as the pitch shot gets longer—in the sixty-yard range—I recommend widening the stance a bit more for lateral stability. Play the ball in the center of your stance, although for chip shots you may want to put it back a little—right of center—to be sure you make solid contact.

The swing begins with the turn of the left shoulder and a swinging of the arms and hands. But as I mentioned in discussing the explosion shot, the hands provide the feel or touch for these shots; they determine how far you will hit the ball, and they create the swing size for the distance. Let me say emphatically, though, that such feel is not something the hands simply have. No one practices the short game enough, and only through practice will the hands "learn" the feel for these shots.

I have developed a specific four-part routine for playing pitch and chip shots:

1. Break the distance down from the edge of the green to the pin into thirds, and *visualize* landing the ball on the first third and rolling it the rest of the way to the hole. I would go so far as to pick a spot *within* that third to land the ball. Naturally, you take into consideration any undulations that may be in the path to the hole and play them accordingly.

2. Choose a club that will do that job. I am hesitant about specifying certain clubs for these shots—for example, an eight-iron if you are a certain distance off the green and the pin is so far back. You may get a different kind of shot with an eight-iron than someone else, in terms of loft and run. Here again, you must practice to find out for yourself what club to use for each situation. It is a matter of trial and error. Ideally, you want the ball to land on the putting surface because you will then get the truest bounce. But there are situations where you cannot do that; if, for instance, you are twenty feet off the green and there is very little green from the edge of the green to the cup, and fringe you are playing over is low-cut and firm, you might want to land the ball short of the green.

3. Visualize the ball as landing and running to the hole. Take a couple of practice swings to rehearse what you have visualized for the total distance and how much swing you feel you need for that distance. Think of the target when you begin those practice swings.

4. Set up at the ball and execute the shot with a picture in your mind's eye of where you want the ball to end up. *Mind's eye* is the key term here. It is essential that you *visualize* all aspects of these shots. That is more important to success than the mechanics of hitting the ball. Why? Because there are four ways to let your right side beat you on these shots, in particular on the pitches.

If your backswing is too short or too slow, your right side will jump at the ball. If your backswing is too fast, your left side will decelerate in the impact zone and the right side will take over the action. If the backswing is too long, the same deceleration effect will occur; the right hand will slap at the ball. When the right side has taken over, the clubhead usually passes the hands before the ball is hit. The right size and speed of the swing are essential to these shots, and they are arrived at best through visualization.

I do not think of starting with the left shoulder on short pitches, putts, chips, and bunker shots; I think only of the target.

Putting

It is said by many golf teachers that the putting stroke is simply a miniature version of the full swing. I agree, as long as the full swing is an effective one. I believe my basic swing system will produce the best possible

Putting. The open position I advocate (top left) for playing full-swing golf shots applies also to putting. So does the one move that starts the swing or stroke. Being open at address gives you a good look at the line of the putt, but also encourages taking the club back on a straight line. Cross-handed putting, illustrated by Tom Kite (lower left) and Fred Couples, is the best way to achieve left-hand dominance and right-hand passivity in this very delicate part of the game.

Shaping Shots and the Short Game **119**

putting stroke. This confidence stems from the open shoulders and hips in the address position that I advocate, and the swinging of the arms, hands, and shoulders to start the swing.

In the case of putting, being open at address allows you a good look at the line you have chosen to putt on. It also helps you to take the club back on a straight line from the ball. In putting there *are* straight lines in the swing, at least for the short ones. A pretty good reference to how good this position can be for putting is Jack Nicklaus, perhaps the greatest putter the game has ever had, especially under pressure. The stance I teach is not quite as open as his, but the effect is the same.

By concentrating on starting the stroke with the swinging of the arms, hands, and shoulders as one unit, you should have no torso movement. Also, because the shoulders still turn at right angles to your spine, you will remain centered.

I really believe that more and more people in years to come will putt cross-handed—that is, with the left hand below the right hand. It suits my basic system, because the dominant left hand/arm creates a better radius. Also, the right arm is more bent and passive and will not overpower the left. Consider that three of the top ten players in the world in 1993 putted cross-handed—Bernhard Langer, Tom Kite, and Fred Couples. Two U.S. Opens have been won by cross-handed putters: Orville Moody in 1969 and Tom Kite in 1992.

Whether or not you putt cross-handed, I think the reverse-overlap grip is best—that is, the index finger of the left (or right) hand rides across the last two fingers of the right (or left) hand. For the conventional putter, it is the best grip to keep the left hand dominant in the stroke. For putting, just as in the rest of the game, a passive right side is essential to success.

Otherwise, the hands are in a neutral position with palms facing each other—the back of the left hand faces the target; the back of the right hand faces opposite the target. For putting, I suggest only one departure in the grip from the standard. The club should lie in between the heel and thumb pads of the right (or left) hand. And your weight should favor the left side at address.

The stroke begins with a swinging of the arms, hands, and shoulders. The best putting stroke is made with the big muscles of the arms, hands, and shoulders all working as much as a single unit as possible.

CHAPTER FIVE

Playing the Game

I don't think it is necessary to go on warning you that when on the golf course playing a round you should not—must not—be thinking about all the different mechanics of the golf swing and the setup. Starting the swing with your left shoulder is all you should be relating to, but this is an uncomplicated idea; it is, in fact, the one and only swing key you should have when playing poorly or well. It is especially valuable when you are nervous about your match or whatever the competitive format may be. The left-shoulder move will let you make a good swing when you are nervous, because it doesn't have the same physiological nerve structure of the hands and arms. Fear or nervousness eliminates feel, and if your heart is pumping under pressure you want to go with something that will overcome that tension. The move of the left shoulder is just the ticket.

Otherwise, on the golf course you have to trust your setup and the first move and concentrate on *playing the game*. That involves strategy, reading greens, visualizing each shot, and finding ways to keep relaxed.

Managing Your On-Course Game

CHOOSING THE RIGHT SHOT

Many years ago when I played in the North-South Amateur championship, I met and became friends with Dudley Wysong. At that time he told me of a conversation he had had with Byron Nelson having to do with how to manage your game from day to day. Nelson said that you should go with what you are doing that day. In other words, if you are hooking the ball, play the hook. If you are cutting the ball, play the cut. Well, if Byron Nelson said that, then it must be right, and I played golf that way for many years. I don't know why it took me so long to realize it didn't work for me, but it didn't. I had never liked playing that way and finally devised my own way to deal with what is a very common situation in golf.

I decided that the best way to counter the fact that I happened to be hooking the ball on a particular day, or vice versa, was to try to hit the ball the opposite way. However, because I had also determined that the best golf was played when you did not think about swing mechanics during the round, I realized that when I practiced I should always hit shots that curved from right to left and left to right; I also threw in some straight balls. The idea was to put into my body memory the feeling of hitting those types of shots so that when I needed them on the golf course I could visualize the shot and let my body memory take over.

That is not quite as simple as it sounds. For instance, it may just happen that hitting a hook is harder for you than hitting a cut shot. There is no explaining it; it is just the way it is. Therefore, when you are having a day when you are cutting the ball from left to right too much and you need a shot that curves from right to left—a hook or draw—you must visualize that shot all the harder. I have a number scale I use. If I need a hook and that is a hard shot for me to do, I visualize it many more times than I would a cut shot. And if there is a big obstacle I have to hook the ball around, I add a few more visualizations. It may come to six or eight hook visualizations. Which means, I look at the shot before me, then in my mind visualize many times in succession hitting a ball that curves from right to left. I burn that flight pattern into my mind. I may need even more visualizations of that shot if the wind is coming from left to right, which would counter a hooking ball. I might have to add a few more visualizations if I'm also playing off a sloping lie with the ball below my feet, which tends to produce a left-to-right flight. I may have to visualize the shot twenty times or more to recall the body reaction that I want and need to pull it off.

Why is this better than simply playing the trajectory you happen to be hitting on a certain day? Why not just aim more to the right if you are hooking? Because, for one thing, by doing so you are giving in to a weakness. If you let it take over your game, you will find it all the more difficult to get it out of your game.

In another scene from this play, let's say the last shot you hit was badly hooked and now you have a shot off a right-to-left slope—a hook stance—and the wind is also blowing from right to left. You could just play the ball farther out to the right to allow for the fact that you are already hooking the ball and are playing under conditions that also foster a hook, but you are going to be anxious about that shot—fearful that you will hook it too much. Chances are you will hit a poor shot, hook or otherwise, because you have the previous shot still in your memory bank. In a case like this, you want to be able to visualize a cut shot, even off a hook stance, to put the ball on or close to your target. The whole idea of working the opposite side of the street, so to speak, in countering your tendency to hook by cutting the ball is to work yourself back to neutral in your swing and into a more positive attitude.

There is another kind of course-management decision that is commonly made, which I believe is wrong. Let's say there is trouble on the right for a fairly long approach shot to a green. The usual advice given by golf teachers and in instruction books is to aim away from the trouble and try to curve the ball back toward your target. But what if there is also trouble on the left, as there usually is? You don't want to be in the woods on the left any more than you want to be in the water to the right, so the swing you eventually make is going to be tight and uncertain. The better play is to go into your body memory bank and visualize a slight cut shot—a two-visualization cut, say—starting the ball at the left corner of the green and well right of the trouble on that side of the hole.

The same visualization idea works for hitting the ball higher or lower than normal. If you are a low-ball hitter and have to hit one high, visualize that higher shot. You will automatically move the ball a bit more forward in your stance and do whatever else you do to get it up—things you learned to do on the practice tee, where you fed your body the feel for the shot you needed. Just how many visualizations each individual needs for each situation is a personal thing and comes out of experience. Some people may need more or fewer visualizations to get enough hook or cut in their body for the shot before them. In any case, the visualizations don't take very long. You can make sixteen or twenty visualizations of a hook or cut shot or high ball or whatever in ten seconds—just knock them off one right after the other.

This concept of visualization does not relate only to shots in which there is trouble to be avoided in a particular circumstance. It can be used to regain a positive attitude, to reduce the potential for anxiety and improve your shot making during the course of a round without trying to make swing changes or corrections. Let's say on the first tee you push your drive to the right into some rough. It is not a terrible shot, but you know you don't want to keep hitting the ball to the right off the tee because it will eventually get you into real trouble. In other words, you do not want to make the same mistake two times in a row because that will weaken your confidence. Your body has a way of remembering what it did the first time; it maintains the feeling of the last shot, which in your hypothetical case was a push to the right. So, on the next tee where you are using your driver you visualize hitting a hook. That doesn't mean you stand there and aim to the right and try to curve the ball from right to left. What you are doing is countering by means of visualization the feeling of that push to the right you hit the last time. The shot you actually hit may not be a hook at all; it will probably be a dead straight shot. But it won't be a push to the right.

This approach to the next shot after a poor one has the effect of allaying anxiety; it gives you hope, and in golf you have to have a lot of hope. If you walk up to the next driver shot after hitting the previous one to the right and you have nothing in your mind to help you avoid repeating that mistake, you will repeat the mistake.

CLUBBING FOR DISTANCE

Picking the right club for shots is one of the most vital elements in game management. Golfers spend as much time finding out how much yardage they have as they do on how they want to swing the club. A lot of poor shots are the result of uncertainty about club selection. I have a routine for picking the club that works well for me. But before getting into that or any other club-selection routine, you have to know how far *on average* you hit with each club in your bag. The only way to find that out is on the practice tee, hitting twenty or thirty shots with each club. Out of that bunch of shots you will come up with a range, a primary distance, which will be determined by where most of the balls have clustered. You don't take the longest shots or the shortest ones as your gauge, but the middle-range cluster. That's your average distance with each club. With that knowledge fixed in your mind, you have the basis for your club-selection decisions on the golf course.

There are a few steps to follow.

1. Get the yardage for the shot you have to play.

2. Assess the lie. Is the ball sitting in some thick grass that will probably get between the clubface and ball at impact and cause the ball to come out with little spin? If so, the ball is going to go farther than normal; much of the extra distance will be in the form of roll. Or, is the ball on some tight turf where you can nip it and put a lot of spin on it? If you are playing off a downhill slope, figure you will hit the ball a little lower and not as far in the air. If you have an uphill lie, the ball will fly higher and go farther. Evaluate your lie.

3. Consider the surface of the ground where you plan to land the ball. Is it firm, or soft? Put this information into your computer.

4. Which way is the wind blowing and how hard is it blowing? This is a major concern in club selection.

5. Are you shooting downhill or uphill? If downhill, the shot will always play a little less long than the actual distance. Depending on the degree of slope, it could be as much as fifteen yards shorter than the actual yardage. And if the shot is uphill, it will play longer than the actual yardage. Also, if you have a large sand trap in front of the green that is twenty or thirty yards from front to back, it will trick your eye and make the shot to the pin look closer than it actually is. The same thing is true when you are playing over a large

body of water. In each case, you need precise yardage to the pin in order to choose the right club for the shot.

Finally, after feeding all that information into your system, visualize the kind of shot you want to play. Then, look at the ground at the target site, as this will fine-tune your picture and further help you pick the right club. And by all means, once you have made your decision, go with it in full confidence. You will then make your best swing.

The advice that you should be confident of your decision brings to mind another aspect of club selection that also bears on the tempo and mental attitude you bring to your shot making. I relate it to the shot we all come up with once in a while, where a tree is directly behind your ball and your backswing is restricted. Most golfers will stand there and keep making practice swings to see how far back they can go before hitting the tree with their club. They will bop that tree with their club a number of times. And although the room they have behind the ball never changes, they keep making that practice swing. In doing so they become too mechanical when they finally come to hitting the ball. As a result, they seldom get the most out of the shot. The solution is to make one practice swing, which will tell you how far back you can take the club, then go ahead and hit the ball.

Now, that very same process—what I call putting the tree on it—should be used when playing all shots, even standard ones from good lies in the fairway. Once you have gone through your club-selection process and visualized your shot, you don't need to go through that process again. If you keep going over all the details you will get tight and lose your athletic spontaneity. Golf is a difficult game in part because there is so little natural spontaneity in it. You don't react to anything in golf the way you do in tennis or baseball or most other sports, and you have to find small ways to achieve that because it helps produce a good flow of action. Every golf shot begins from a standstill, and the more times you consider your decision and the longer you stand over your ball before starting the swing, the more difficult it is to achieve any degree of athletic spontaneity.

With this in mind, I also don't like to figure out my shot too far in advance of my turn to play. For one thing, the conditions may change and then I have to go through the process again, which can break up my playing rhythm. I recommend going through the process as close to your turn to play as you can, so that you can move right into the shot itself. The tempo of your play will be better, as will the shots.

CLUBBING UP

Another area of course management in regard to clubbing that is important to consider is, if you're not hitting the ball with much power on a given day take a little less club for each shot, especially when you have a less-than-perfect lie. If the shot calls for a three-wood, go down to the five-wood. There isn't as much difference in distance between the two clubs as you might think, and because you will probably hit the five-wood solidly you may very well reach your target anyway. You should know that there is an eight- to ten-yard difference between each club *for golfers who can hit a driver in the 250-yard range*, and only a three- to four-yard differential for less-powerful golfers. Golfers who don't know that will make a poor decision in the fairway, taking a club with not enough loft for a poor lie because they want the extra yardage.

The best game management is that which encourages a solidly struck shot, which almost invariably comes when you swing within yourself.

DEALING WITH WEATHER

One of the many things that makes golf so fascinating and complex a game is that it is played in all sorts of weather conditions. As the Scots like to say about golf on their links courses, if you have no wind you have no golf. In any case, you must deal with various weather conditions in order to get the most out of your game, and the following are some tips I have developed over the years.

COLD WEATHER

As you know, most of your body heat is lost through your head, so it is important to wear a hat in cold weather. In fact, I often wear two hats at the same time—actually a thin wool watch cap under a regular golf cap or hat.

Thermal underwear is excellent for keeping warm without feeling, or actually being, bundled up; it allows you to swing freely. You can wear a short-sleeved golf shirt over the thermal underwear to help reduce the bundled-up feeling even more. The bottom line in all this is you don't want to wear things that will restrict your swing.

For the hands, I recommend rain mittens or a waterproof cart glove that has a coating on it. The mitten is much better than a fingered glove, because you can get in and out of it much more easily and it also allows your fingers to be together inside, which gets them warmer more quickly.

I also wear two pairs of socks—a thin pair underneath the usual, heavier golf socks. And if you are playing out of a cart, which makes it all the colder, bring along a big coat that you can get in and out of easily; wear it in between shots. Either way, keep on the move between shots; don't stand in one place. And if you can, share the cart driving with your partner and walk every other hole, or half of each hole.

As for shot making itself in cold weather, know that the ball does not travel as far as it does in warmer air. You will have to take at least one more club for the distance than you would normally use. Cold air is heavier than warm air and, when it blows, the flight of the ball encounters even more resistance. A little bit of cold wind acts like a lot of warm wind. A 5-mph wind in the cold is equivalent to around a 15-mph wind in warm weather. Finally, the greens are usually harder and crustier and you will have to allow for the ball running farther after it lands.

HOT WEATHER

To my mind, golf is best when it is warm and even hot. The ball goes farther, and your body is looser. There are no tricks to the shot making in hot weather, but you do have to take care of your body. It is vital that you drink a lot of water. I remember what an old pro once told me about playing in hot weather: Never pass a water fountain without taking a drink, otherwise you'll wilt like a flower. If it is very humid, you have to move more slowly.

PLAYING IN THE RAIN

The most important thing about playing in the rain is keeping your grips dry. You should have a towel under the hood covering your clubs, to keep it dry for wiping your hands between shots. You might also hang a towel on the spokes under your umbrella, but be careful not to get it wet when you put the umbrella on the ground.

I don't usually play with a glove except in the rain, because as soon as I feel the club may slip I will grip it tighter and restrict my release in the impact zone. The same thing happens to everyone. In this regard, I suggest keeping a lot of your old gloves in a waterproof bag for rainy days. If you have enough of them, and the rain is really steady, you can change gloves after every shot.

Rain causes more problems in shot making than any other condition of play. It is harder to get the ball properly airborne because of the moisture on it, and because you can impart less spin to it at impact. A four-wood will play like a three-wood, for example, but the difference can be as much as three clubs, depending on the lie. When playing out of longish wet grass, you will very likely get moisture between the clubface and ball at impact, which causes what is known as a "flyer"—the ball shooting out with very little spin and going much farther than it would ordinarily. In wet weather it is especially important to read your lie to get an estimate of how the ball will come out of it.

Reading Greens

The key to reading greens is knowing how the green tilts. That may be obvious, but I find many golfers who totally misread or fail altogether to ascertain the basic slope of greens. There are two ways to read the green accurately. One is before you even step onto the putting surface. It is easier to see how a green tilts or banks from a distance than when you are standing on it, so as you approach the green scan the entire surface to see if it is higher on the right or left, if it is higher at the rear than in front, or both.

Once on the green, I have found it valuable to look at fellow golfers if they are at a distance from me. If I know they are the same height as I am, for instance, but they appear shorter, then I know the green is higher where I am standing and the green breaks down toward them. If they appear taller, then of course the green slopes up toward them. I often have my caddie walk to the other side of the green from where I am standing to get this reading.

I also think it is valuable to look from the hole back to the ball to gauge distance. When walking back to the ball from the hole, I believe in staying some five yards away from the line of putt to get a better perspective from which to see any slope that may be there. Looking from the side of the line of putt also gives you a reading on the break, as well as tells you whether you are going uphill or downhill. I make my final reading of the putt from eight feet behind the ball, looking at the hole. In the old days they would tell you to get down right behind the ball for this reading, but it is much better to get farther back, again for better perspective.

I also look inside the hole itself. The side that has the most dirt showing between the edge of the hole and the top of the plastic or metal liner is the high side; the side with the least dirt is the low side.

When you are playing in the afternoon on greens with a lot of grain, such as Bermuda grass that is common in the south, it is wise to know which way is west or southwest because the grass grows during the day and the blades turn toward the setting sun. In Florida this is especially important, because the Bermuda grasses grown there are very sturdy and the grain definitely influences how fast your ball will run and in what direction. Remember, on grainy greens the ball will roll towards the tips of grass blades. And of course, if you are putting into those tips, the putt will be slower; putting with the tips gives a faster roll.

Northern grasses aren't as grainy as the grasses used on most southern courses. But there may be some grain, and because it is a finer blade it will be harder to read than the grain on southern Bermuda grass. Generally, northern grasses grow downhill. Otherwise, because it is against the rules to brush the grass on the green itself with your putter or with your hand to see which way the grain is growing, brush the fringe grass nearby, which is legal; the grain on it will be the same for your putt.

On the longer putts I break the distance down into segments. If it is a sixty-footer, for example, I divide it into three twenty-footers; a forty-footer into two twenty-footers. This helps you make a better reading of both distance and slope. However, be aware that the last segment is the most important because by then the ball is slowing down and any slope in the green will have a greater effect.

After reading the green and lining up the putt, I like to make my practice strokes beside the ball *while looking at the hole, not the ball*. I do this in order to get my mind off the stroke and onto the target. I want to be completely target oriented, not stroke or ball conscious, so that the stroke will not be rushed, forced, or mechanically directed. It is the same thing as when pitching pennies to a wall; you look at the wall, not the penny in your hand. This gives you a sense of the speed and size of the swing you need to pitch the penny or hit your putt.

How do you judge the speed of a green? You can't *see* how fast a green is, except perhaps by watching how the putts of other players in your group travel. But you never really know how well or poorly they hit the ball, or their personal sense of a green's speed. Reading the speed of a green is just that, strictly a sensory understanding and a very personal one. It is a key to good putting because it determines how hard or soft you must hit your putt, but it is not in any way a tangible factor the way grain is. You get a sense of the speed of a green through your feet, by simply walking on the putting surface. And you will have hit some putts on the practice putting green before the round; if the practice green is a good one—which is to say, it matches the greens on the course—you will have a somewhat more concrete feel for the speed. And that's about it for reading the speed. But what do you do about it? What does that tell you about how hard you should hit the ball?

With the information on speed worked into my sensory system, I like to articulate to myself in actual language the distance I have to go. In this way I am giving myself a kind of history lesson. The mind remembers what you have done under similar conditions in the past, and that memory or experience can be called up and used again. You remember how hard you hit a forty-footer on fairly fast greens, or a sixteen-footer on slow ones, and by saying the distance the body memory kicks in and you have a sense of how hard you must hit the ball.

If you were to say to yourself, hit the ball harder because it's a forty-footer and the green is slow, you are too conscious of what you are doing or have to do. You will become mechanical. You have an intrinsic frame of reference taken from current and past experience, and you must trust that your instincts will produce a good putt out of that information. Putting is a fine art; it is more art than science, and you have to approach it more with a sense of feel than mechanics. If you get too conscious of what you must do, you are like the centipede who has been asked to explain how he walks. A good putt is made with a swing of the club, and if you are trying to control that movement by saying hit it hard or hit it soft, you are not going to make a *swing*. A swing has to be a subconscious reaction to information you have ingested and, in a sense, forgotten. With every putt you write a story. There is the line, the slope, the speed, etc.—the details of the story. But when you come to put it down on paper, so to speak, you don't think about all the details; you try to find the essence of the story. In the end, that is what putting comes down to.

COLLARED?

There are times when your ball comes to rest on the edge of the green and up against the second cut of fringe. You are on the collar, with the grass higher behind the ball than in front of it. It is a troublesome shot, but there are ways to play it successfully:

1. Use your putter and more or less chip the ball. With an open stance, play the ball behind the right foot, and in the stroke break your wrists and hands immediately and hit down on the center of the ball.

If the ball is actually in the collar, or second cut, and sitting down in the grass, this stroke will pop the ball out and get it rolling.

2. Use your four-wood or five-wood and putt it. Play the ball in your stance as you would normally. The weight of the club and the broad sole will help it slide through the heavy grass behind the ball and put a good roll on it. However, if the ball is down a little deeper in the grass, play it back a bit more in your stance and open your feet.

WALKING LOOSE

When walking between shots, or even on the way to the golf course, I like to do so with my hips loose. This relaxes the back muscles in particular and allays overall tension. Many golfers relieve tension by shaking their hands lightly, but I don't think this is especially worthwhile. Everything to do with the motion required for the golf swing involves muscles that are directly or indirectly connected to the hips. They are the key to keeping loose. Also, being in torso alignment at address promotes looseness, because the arms are not stretching out away from the body. Stretching, or reaching for the ball at address, is a tension-creating position.

KEEPING AWAY UNTIL IT'S TIME

I don't think it's a good idea to stand close to your ball while you are waiting to play your shot. You are apt to overanalyze your situation—the yardage, the lie, how important the shot is to your match or score. This builds unnecessary and destructive tension and lends itself to second-guessing yourself. Stay ten or so yards away from the ball until it's your turn to play, then walk up to the ball, get your distance, assess your lie, make a decision on how you want to play the shot and with what club, then go on and do it.

CHAPTER SIX

Playing the Mind Game

In talking about the mental side of playing golf, I don't feel I am getting into an area that I am not qualified to discuss. While the sports psychologists do bring to their work some special training that most golf professionals don't have, they are for the most part gaining a lot of their insights from their work with golf professionals who are very thoughtful about the game and have a very intense daily experience with it. Furthermore, a lot of what I teach is in the area of feel rather than mechanics, and that naturally falls into the mental side of golf. So, I want to add some of my thoughts to this highly important part of playing the game—a part that has been estimated by most professionals to consist of at least 80 percent of the energy used in one round of golf. I have broken my thoughts down into particular areas.

Patience

We hear tour golfers use the word *patience* a lot when they are interviewed on tournament telecasts . . . and it is in truth perhaps the most essential attribute of good golf. The result of patience is an overall calmness of mind that allows you to coordinate physically to the best of your ability. There are a lot of things that happen during a round of golf that can make you impatient. For example, the people in your group don't behave the way you think they should—they are not courteous and talk while you are preparing for your shots; your caddie is not doing a good job; you get a bad bounce. Or, you simply cannot hit shots the way you planned. The latter is the one that often gets you into the worst trouble, because you seek to fix your swing on the course during the round in order to make your shots come off. But in so doing, you become swing conscious and distract yourself from playing the game.

Actually, trying to fix your swing on the course is next to impossible because you don't hit enough shots in succession to find out if you've done it. But sometimes you find a key, some move or other that produces a better strike of the ball, and an odd thing often happens in this case. You may fix your swing and begin to flight the ball very well—hit solid shots—but they end up in trouble because you didn't *play* them right. If you're trying to figure out the jigsaw puzzle of the golf swing at the same time as you are trying to make a good score, chances are you will not integrate all the other playing factors—such as the wind, the lie, the distance—that are integral to playing the game. This is where patience comes in. You have to be able to wait out the poor shots and bad luck, to cope with the problems but try not to solve them at that moment. That is the key to golf—and life, too, when you think about it. Impatiently trying to fix your swing in the middle of a round is like a young child wanting to know if you are there yet.

When things aren't going well during a round of golf, you have to keep trying with the tools you have brought to the game that day. After the round is over is when you work out the swing problems, out on the practice tee.

Poise

Poise is the ability to concentrate under pressure, to think the clear thoughts you need to make good shots or good decisions. Poise is going through your checklist, your routine before each shot. You don't think about what the shot means—its importance to the competition—you make yourself stick to the basics of your shot-making pattern.

Golfers can get too emotional not only when things go badly on the course, but also when they are going well. Poise is not letting either happen. One thing I do when things are not going well during a round is to withdraw from the golf course mentally and consider what is *really* important in life. For me, it is my Christianity. Because of the nature of golf, it seems that there is no mistake you make in your office or any bad business deal you are involved in that is as discouraging as hitting a poor golf shot—especially while under pressure. It's more dramatic, everyone can see the flop, it's a hard thing for the ego to handle. But if you can somehow withdraw from the game, be rational and put the event in a larger perspective, you can get through it. After all, it *is* only a game. You hit a bad shot, but you are still alive and kicking; no one is going to fire you; you have your health. You anchor yourself to something bigger than the game, and a bogey pales into insignificance, which is where it truly belongs. I call that having poise—the ability to change your focus and be anchored to something besides golf even as you continue to play your game, not to be overpowered by golf-course events to the extent that you lose your sense of the larger reality.

Objectivity

You have to play golf with a realistic assessment of your abilities. You can't evaluate yourself and make decisions based on your best shots. You aren't as good as your best shot. That's like a bowler who throws ten games, with his best a 300, who then evaluates himself as a 300 bowler—or, the golfer who thinks his practice-tee golf is what he can count on on the course. On the practice tee you are hitting one ball after another from the same lie, with the same club, with the same foot position and target line. What happens is that you begin to think you will automatically hit it on the golf course just as well. A lot of golfers do that kind of thing, which leaves them open for a fall. You have to consider that you are as good as your medium shots. That's being objective. The result is, you won't be trying to hit low-percentage shots that you have not been successful with or haven't practiced a lot. You can't let your best shots be your norm of evaluation. They can be your goal, but not your realistic standard. As Ben Hogan once said, he expected to hit maybe three shots perfectly during a round of golf. Golf is a game of good misses. You have to plan your shots not with your ego but by what you realistically can do.

Self-Evaluation

If you are working on your game—developing some new swing idea—and you have an important round to play the next day, you have to decide if you should bring that swing change with you to the course. How do you make that evaluation? If you are missing the ball a little, not hitting it solidly but the ball is going pretty straight, you must be on plane and catching the ball around the center of the clubface. You don't make any of the changes for the big round. Your timing might just be off a little, so you just hang around and wait for that to improve. It usually does.

By the same token, if you are hitting the ball solidly but off-line, you must be getting pretty good coil. So just wait until something good happens to your game; wait until you begin to straighten out your shots.

On the other hand, if you are mis-hitting and flighting the ball off-line, you have a problem that needs to be worked on; whatever you deem to be the solution is taken to the course. That's self-evaluation.

Energy Conservation

Everyone has only a certain amount of nervous energy in the course of a day. Nervous energy gives you the ability to concentrate fully, to have adrenaline flow when you need it, to stay physically and mentally alert to make good decisions and good swings. Maybe your top energy level is there for forty-five minutes. That's a fairly long time. But an eighteen-hole round of golf takes about four hours, so before you get on the course it is important that you do not use up much or any of your nervous energy in preparing for the round.

On the practice tee, don't hit too many balls, and by all means do not get emotionally involved in making them good shots—or worrying that they aren't good ones. That will only burn up energy you need on the course. If you leak out too much energy on the practice tee, you won't have it where you really need it. I've found it a good idea to program a certain number of practice shots to hit before a round and, regardless of how you hit them—good, bad, or indifferent—do not deviate from that number. Stick to your program; don't get caught up in what the ball is doing on your practice shots.

Qualifying Your Changes

If you are in the process of making one or more changes in your swing, don't take the new idea into an important round or a tournament until it qualifies to get in there—if you feel really secure that it is right and will work under the gun. The qualifying begins on the practice tee. If it works there, you go a few holes or an entire friendly round with it. Then it gets into the big game. To again quote Ben Hogan, the master course and game manager, never try a shot or a swing on the course that you haven't first tried on the practice tee.

Enlarging Your Boundaries

I said earlier that when things are not going well for you on the course you have to be able to put everything in a larger perspective and not take it so seriously that you do not enjoy the game. And yet, you can't really play golf with the mindset of someone out to enjoy yourself the way you do when you go to the beach or to watch a big-league baseball game. There is a fine line here. Playing good golf requires the same mental attitude you bring to your business life. It is a test of will and skill you must pass without submitting to worry, self-pity, jealousy, bitterness, and other such bad attitudes that only mire you deeper in the swamp of discontent.

The way to this positive, optimistic attitude is by constantly seeking to improve your golf swing and the quality of the shots you are hitting. The golf swing is a giant jigsaw puzzle that you may spend a lot of your life putting together. But that's one of the great fascinations of golf. It takes time and effort to work on the mechanics of the swing, to improve them, and then to make them work under pressure and with any club in the bag. Finally, you expand the art by learning to hit different types of shots—draws, hooks, cuts, slices, high and low ones. There are so many permutations within those basic areas, and you should never be satisfied until you can hit them all. Some types of shots may be more suited to your swing than others, but you should not give up the idea of learning to hit all shots. That keeps your swing honest and is a good way to improve your overall swing action. Expanding your boundaries in this way will carry over to your mental attitude and everything else that impacts on your game.

Humility

The Bible says arrogance brings a man low, that pride comes before a fall, and God lifts up the humble. I don't mean to sermonize here, but I think there is a correlation between those words and your approach to golf. In a word, you are better off with a certain sense of humility rather than arrogance. By humility I don't mean standing round-shouldered with your head down at a presentation and saying that your win was really nothing.

Humility is the ability to be thankful for your talent and gifts, and especially being aware that you are not an island and your success came with the help of other people and other things—good luck in the genetics derby, parents and friends who supported you emotionally and financially, a teacher or two who gave you vital information on how to play.

Humility can be a state of self-confidence and might appear arrogant, but the difference is that the self-confident person realizes there were a lot of factors outside of himself that contributed to his success. Arrogance is thinking that you and you alone are responsible for your success. But by thinking this way you are always on stage and defensive about how you perform in front of others. To bring that down to the nitty-gritty of a round of golf, or your attitude in a longer competition, an arrogant person must always defend his or her ability, which adds a lot of pressure—constant pressure. Humility, as I define it, breeds relaxation.

CHAPTER SEVEN

Equipment and Your Game

Shafts

I don't have a special recipe for what kind of equipment you should use for my swing ideas, because the two things don't relate in that way. That is not to say choosing the right equipment is not important, and I want to get into a few aspects of it that I think are especially important, in particular the shaft you use in your clubs. The shaft is the heart of the golf club—the single most important factor.

First of all, I don't believe swing speed should be the central criterion for selecting the shaft flex for your clubs. That is what many club fitters base their judgment on. For one thing, just knowing your swing speed can spook you—it does me. I don't know my swing speed and don't want to know. All knowing it can do is lessen your self-confidence, at least if your swing speed is relatively slow. Your swing speed is what it is, and tests have shown that no matter how much you improve the mechanics of your swing or what type of shaft you use, you can't increase your natural swing speed more than a couple of miles per hour.

Besides, swing speed doesn't tell you what kind of spin or angle of trajectory you get on the ball, which are factors just as influential as the speed itself in determining how far you can hit a ball and what type of shaft you should use to get that distance. To use a football analogy, a quarterback who throws the ball seventy yards is throwing it higher than when he throws it twenty yards, but his arm speed in both cases may be exactly the same. Only his launch angle is different.

There is also the matter of release time, which swing speed has little to do with. How late or early do you release or uncock your wrists in the impact zone? If you swing the club at 90 mph but release it late and keep the loft on the club low, you won't hit it as high as when you have an earlier release with the same swing speed but hit it higher. So I've always gauged shaft-flex selection by how far a person can naturally hit a ball. It's a pretty simple formula: If you can drive the ball 250 yards, you need a stiff shaft. If you drive it 220 to 230 yards, you are borderline between stiff and regular. And if you are in that category and go to stiff, you'd better have a club in the D-3 swing-weight area and with some loft on it to kick the ball in the air. If you hit the ball under 220 yards, then you should use an r-flex shaft.

I think that the stiffer the shaft you can use, the better off you are *providing you can get it to flex properly at impact*. A stiff shaft will give you more control and power. Why pull a ten-pound bow if you can use a twenty-pound one? But don't let your ego get in your way on this. Thinking that you have to use a stiff shaft in your driver to drive the ball farther is foolish and we are seeing less of it. As a matter of fact, most golfers should be using shafts in the r-range, including pros, and we are seeing a trend in that direction.

The best way to find out what shaft flex is right for you is to hit balls on the range. Indeed, that's the only way to get any aspect of club fitting done; you have to see how the ball flies to know what is right. If you have to muscle a shaft, you will feel it. By that I mean you will instinctively try to hit the ball harder, because you will sense the need to do so. The ball will probably fly on a lower trajectory than you want or would ordinarily get. If the shaft is too soft, or whippy, you will feel that too; and you will hit a lot of upshooters and floaters that don't go very far. You will also spray many balls off target.

In the old days in golf, getting a shaft flex was pretty easy; you had four choices—extra stiff, stiff, regular, and ladies'. Now many manufacturers aren't even going with those designations, instead putting numbers on their shafts to indicate flexibility that reflects their own measurement system. There is also an emphasis now on flex point, that place on the shaft where the most flex occurs. Theoretically, a low flex or kick point, which is usually recommended for less-powerful hitters, will hit the ball higher; a high flex point is usually recommended for harder hitters, because they need more control. However, the actual difference between a high and a low flex point on shafts is about an inch or an inch and a half, and quite frankly I don't see that as making a lot of difference one way or the other. Try out shafts with different flex characteristics; forget what the numbers or letters the manufacturers put on the shafts say, and discover for yourself which works best for you.

A word about graphite shafts, which are becoming more and more popular: For all the technological advances that have been made in graphite shafts over the past ten years, the manufacturing process is still not that precise and you have to spend a lot of time and money to get a complete set of clubs with graphite shafts that match up correctly in flexibility and weight. And even if you get them just right, you aren't going to hit the ball any farther than with steel shafts. That's what most golfers think, that graphite is going to give them more yardage, but you have to be a 250-yard hitter to get 7 more yards with graphite. If you are not as long a hitter, naturally, the increase you get with graphite scales down quite a bit. The real advantage to graphite is it is easier on the bones, tendons, and joints because it absorbs shock much better than steel.

Club Length

Another trend in equipment has been toward overlong clubs. The standard driver used to be forty-two inches long. But now we are seeing drivers up to forty-five inches long, and I believe that is getting in the danger zone for the average golfer. The point of the longer club is to help hit the ball farther, but the longer the club is the harder it is to control in terms of solid contact and flight accuracy. If you don't make a solid hit you are not going to get the extra yardage anyway, and you will also be playing a lot of shots from bad places on the course. You need to be playing a lot of golf, practicing just as much, and have some special talent for the game in the first place to use a driver in the forty-five-inch-long range. Which brings up another point on this subject: Many golfers are using an extra-long driver, while the rest of their set is standard length. That means making an adjustment in the address position and in the swing that is not going to produce consistent ball striking.

Lie Angle

Lie angle is another important element in club fitting, especially with irons, because lie angle affects how the clubhead will go through the ground when taking a divot. You want the sole of the iron to be flush with the ground at impact. If the lie angle is too upright—the toe of the club well off the ground at address—the heel of the club is going to catch up in the turf when the ball is struck. If the lie angle is too flat—the heel off the ground at address—the toe end of the clubhead, the weakest portion of the club, will make the main contact with the ball and turf, causing a relatively weak shot.

Most irons are to some degree upright in lie angle, and that is as it should be because the shaft of a golf club not only flexes from side to side during the swing, it also bows forward or toes down in the impact zone. Because of the toe-down, you need to have a lie angle that is a little upright. A simple way to get a rough idea of a club's lie angle is to set it in the address position on a smooth floor. If you can slide a quarter under the toe about an inch into the scoring line area, the club has an upright lie angle. Two degrees upright is about standard for most golfers.

Today, using a lie board to hit off is by far the best way to gauge the correct lie angle. Most club fitters use them.

Total Weight

The total weight of a golf club is far more important than its swing weight, yet it is virtually ignored by most golfers. Swing weight is simply the balance factor in a club and doesn't necessarily relate to whether the club is heavy or light enough for you to play effectively. And in recent years, when golfers do get involved in total weight, they have been misled to think that the lighter the club the better because it can be swung faster and thereby will produce more power. The advent of the graphite shaft has propelled this kind of thinking, but it doesn't work that way.

There was one instance I know of where a golfer using a 43.5-inch, 12-ounce driver generated a 100-mph swing speed and carried the ball 235 yards. Then, with a 43-inch, $13^3/4$-ounce driver, he generated a 106-mph swing speed and carried the ball another 10 yards. The reason for this was explained by an exercise physiologist from St. Louis named John Davis. He said that if a person's muscles realize they don't have to work hard (or as hard), they won't. Therefore, with a club that feels light you are apt not to swing it as fast as you would a heavier one. Or, you may slow down with the lighter club just because it feels light and you sense you won't be able to control it. Then, too, because a club feels light you may sense you don't have enough mass to hit the ball as powerfully as you would like, and you swing too hard. That's why you see a lot of golfers these days slashing and slapping at the ball with their hands. The scientific fact is, you have to swing a 12-ounce club faster than a 13-ounce club to generate the same amount of energy.

If a club is too heavy in the head you may let the right side dominate in the forward swing and with an early release throw the club from the top, as the saying goes. If a club is not too heavy you will play more with the grip end, which is another way of saying you will lead with the left hand rather than the right, which is good. Ideally, you want feel the head without the club seeming to be too heavy.

CHAPTER EIGHT

How to Practice, and Find Your Own Solutions to Slumps and Swing Problems

As we know, golf is a lonely game in that we are each totally responsible for our successes and failures on every shot we play. We can't take a lesson from a professional before every round, and when practicing we must find our own way to convert what we've learned into good shots and scores. Here are some ideas on how to practice, how to analyze poor shots, and how to correct them on your own.

Practice Made Worthwhile

Standing on the range, beating out one ball after another without any program, is worthless. If you are not hitting the ball well, you will only make a bad swing worse when you do not have a specific problem or swing idea in mind. For that reason, I believe it is best to determine how many balls you want to hit during a practice session. This puts a kind of pressure on you to make every shot valuable. It helps your concentration, too. Ideally, you should practice in short spurts—hit balls for fifteen or twenty minutes two or three times during the day. Such a schedule is impractical for most average golfers, so if you have only one session make it for no more than an hour and with a set number of balls.

The practice tee is a good place to work on shaping shots that are counter to your natural ball flight. This makes your basic swing healthy. If you are a right-to-left player, try hitting the ball left-to-right. It will get you out of a rut, make the game more interesting, and help you to understand your basic swing better.

If you are having trouble with your swing, don't practice with the longer clubs. You will instinctively try harder to hit with these clubs, and the tension this creates will make you dominate the swings with your right side. The best thing is to practice with the shorter irons—from the seven-iron down, and especially with the pitching wedge. These clubs let you develop ambidexterity and good tempo.

Never practice out of bad lies. Many teachers have said that this is a good way to learn how to play difficult lies, but when you are working on your basic swing, you won't get the right feedback; you will not be sure you have made a good swing, because you will instinctively respond to the lie and make swing adjustments to get the ball out of the lie. You develop a good swing playing out of good lies. Then, when you have poor lies, adjustments will be easier to make.

All the above practice ideas are ideal for getting out of a slump. You need positive results to break out of a slump. Therefore, if you are hitting poorly with your long clubs, practice with the shorter ones to get your confidence back—and vice versa. Why do you hit long clubs poorly and shorter ones better? Or vice versa? That brings me to how you can, on your own, understand where your swing problems are and fix them yourself.

1. **PROBLEM:** **Swing Is Too Vertical**

CLUES: Divots with irons are gouged—too deep. Taking a divot with the driver and skying the ball.

CAUSES:
a. Too much weight on the left side at address.
b. The right shoulder too high.
c. Holding the club in the right palm, not the fingers. The left hand is "weak"—turned too far to the left.
d. The spine is left of center at address.
e. You are standing too close to the ball at address.
f. The right side overpowers the left side in takeaway.

CURES: Correct any or all of the above. Take practice swings with only the left arm. Do any of the left-side drills outlined in Chapter Three.

2. **PROBLEM:** **Sweeping the Ball Too Much**

CLUES: With the driver, the clubhead hits the ground behind the ball; called "drop kicking."

CAUSES:
a. Too much weight on the right side at address.
b. The center is moving up, or to the right, in the backswing.
c. The right arm is lifting too much at the start of the backswing.
d. You are standing too far from the ball at address.
e. The right arm uncocks too early.

CURES:
a. Correct any or all of the above.
b. Make sure the shoulders are open 20 degrees at address, so the swing doesn't get too flat or inside early in the backswing.
c. Start the backswing with the left shoulder.

3. **PROBLEM:** **Hooking**

CLUES: The ball in flight swings sharply to the left and away from the target. Or from the right of target onto it or past it on the left.

CAUSES: **a.** The grip is too strong—the right and left hands are turned too much to the right.
b. The shoulders and hips are not open at address.
c. You aim to the right of your intended target.
d. The right hand rolls over the left too early.

CURES: **a.** Correct any or all of the above.
b. Start the backswing with the upper body moving before the lower body.
c. Do left-side drills.

4. **PROBLEM:** **Slicing**

CLUES: The ball in flight curves sharply to the right, away from the intended target. Or the ball starts left of the target and turns sharply right onto the target line or to the right of it.

CAUSES: **a.** The grip is too weak—either the left or right hand, or both, are turned too much to the left. The club is held in the palm of the right hand.
b. The ball is too far forward in the stance.
c. The right shoulder is too high at address.
d. The center is moving to the left in the backswing, causing a reverse pivot with the weight on the left side at the top of the swing and moving to the right side in the forward swing.

CURES: **a.** Correct any or all of the above.

b. Start the backswing with the left-shoulder turn, not the right arm.

c. Do left-side drills.

5. PROBLEM: Power Loss

CLUES: **a.** Hitting the ball solidly but not getting appropriate distance.

CAUSES: **a.** Physical and psychological tension.

b. The stance is too narrow at address.

CURES: **a.** Make sure you have momentum in the preswing— motion and no thought.

b. Make sure the hips are loose.

c. Check Erectness, Openness, and that the Left shoulder is higher than the right at address. Widen your stance.

d. Don't think during the swing.

e. Do left-side drills.

f. Start with a turn of the left shoulder.

6. PROBLEM: Hitting the Ball Too Low

CLUES: **a.** The ball is flying lower than usual with all clubs.

CAUSES: **a.** The ball is too far back in your stance.

b. You are standing too far from the ball at address.

c. Poor E O L.

d. You are aiming to the right of the target.

           e. The grip is too strong.

           f. The right side overpowers the left in takeaway by raising up. The angle of attack becomes too steep.

CURES: **a.** Correct any or all of the above.

           b. Start the backswing with a turn of your left shoulder.

7. PROBLEM: Hitting the Ball Too High

CLUES: **a.** The ball flies higher than usual with all clubs.

CAUSES: **a.** The right hand uncocks too soon.

           b. Your grip is too weak—your left or right hand or both turned too far to the left.

           c. Body tension at address.

           d. Loss of center downward or to left—your body drops at the start of the backswing or tilts to the left.

           e. Sway to the right and no weight transfer from right to left in the forward swing.

CURES: **a.** Correct any or all of the above.

           b. Develop momentum at address—movement plus no thought.

           c. Start the backswing with the turn of the left shoulder.

8. PROBLEM: Hitting Fat

CLUES: **a.** The club hits the ground behind the ball in the forward swing.

CAUSES: **a.** The ball is too forward in the stance.
           b. Loss of center downward or to the right.
           c. Early release of hands in the forward swing.
           d. Body tension at address.
           e. The right arm takes over at the start of the swing and gets too close to the body.
           f. The upper body initiates forward swing; no weight shift to the left.
           g. The right hand uncocks too soon.

CURES: **a.** Correct any or all of the above.
           b. Loosen up at address with movement and no thought.
           c. Start the backswing with the left shoulder, concentrating on a good coil.
           d. Do left-side drills.

9. PROBLEM: Hitting Thin

CLUES: **a.** Hitting the ball in the middle or near the top with irons and woods; the ball flies on very low trajectory.

CAUSES: **a.** You stand too far from the ball at address.
           b. The ball is too far forward in the stance.
           c. Loss of center upward or to the right.
           d. The shoulder and hips are not open 20 degrees at address.
           e. The right hand uncocks too soon.

CURES: **a.** Correct any or all of the above.
           b. Start the backswing with the left-shoulder turn.
           c. Do left-side drills.

10. PROBLEM: Topping the Ball

CLUES: **a.** The ball never gets airborne.

CAUSES: **a.** Loss of center in any direction.
                b. You stand too far from the ball at address.
                c. The ball is too far forward at address.
                d. You think about hitting the ball.
                e. You hold the club in the palm of the right hand, instead of the fingers.
                f. Your right side overpowers the left in forward swing, causing a casting of club—uncocking the right hand too soon.

CURES: **a.** Correct any or all of the above.
                b. Think only of starting the swing with the turn of the left shoulder.
                c. Do left-side drills, making sure to contact the ground with the clubhead.

11. PROBLEM: Shanking

CLUES: **a.** The ball goes straight right off the shank of the club (only with irons).

CAUSES: **a.** Your weight is on your toes at address.
                b. The right shoulder is too high at address.
                c. There is not enough coil of your upper body in the backswing.
                d. Your upper right side dominates the start of the forward swing and your body center moves toward the ball.

e. The swing begins with the hands or the hands and hips, not an upper-body turn.

CURES: **a.** Correct any or all of the above.

b. On the practice tee put a plastic golf ball or any other object—a broomstick, say—about a finger width outside the toe of the club. Do whatever is necessary not to hit the outside object.

c. Crimp your right arm at address to subjugate your right side.

d. To avoid fear of the shot, concentrate on starting the swing with a turn of the left shoulder.

e. Do left-side drills between each practice shot.

12. PROBLEM: Toe Hits

CLUES: **a.** A weak, hooked shot.

CAUSES: **a.** Aiming to the right of the target.

b. Body tension at address.

c. The ball is too far forward at address.

d. You stand too far from the ball at address.

e. Loss of center to right.

f. Poor posture (Erectness).

g. Uncocking the right hand too soon—"slapping" it.

CURES: **a.** Correct any or all of the above.

b. Think only of starting the backswing with a turn of the left shoulder.

c. Do left-side drills.

13. PROBLEM: Heel Hits

CLUES:
    a. Weak shots to the right of the target.
    b. Grounders to the left with woods.

CAUSES:
    a. Loss of center forward toward the ball.
    b. Poor posture (Erectness).
    c. You stand too close to the ball at address.
    d. Your left shoulder and hips are not open at address.
    e. All shank causes could apply.

CURES:
    a. Correct any or all of the above.
    b. Do left-side drills.
    c. Refer to shank cures.

CHAPTER NINE

In Conclusion

There are some underlying themes in my teaching that were not expressed explicitly earlier in this book because I think it is important that you first be given specific techniques. Now is the time to expand upon those techniques and put them in a large context. I would like you to understand that in my teaching, the golf *swing* is not a series of positions taken by various parts of the body—the left arm here, the right knee there, the angle of the plane such and such. That kind of teaching has long been the norm in golf instruction and seems even more popular today. Walk along the practice tee at any pro tour stop, or the teaching stalls at your local driving range, and you will see the so-called swing gurus and everyday, hardworking golf professionals putting their students' arms in this position or that, turning their torsos one way or another, dealing in unequivocal positions. I do not believe that is the way to make a golf swing, and it is certainly not the way to *play* golf. When I say the hands should not get close to the body at the beginning of the backswing, I am not saying they should be so many inches or feet from the body; I am not dictating a position. I am giving a description of what should happen, *approximately*, during the swing.

I do not want my students to think in terms of *inswing* positions, for to do so is to be a stiff, tension-ridden golfer. This is not to say I don't teach any positions at all. I most certainly do. But all of them are in the setup and are in place before the swing begins. That is an important distinction—one that is at the heart of my teaching.

I will take that notion even farther. In my view of the golf swing and the teaching of it there are two main elements: form and style. Form is E O L and Center, Radius, Plane, and Coil. Style is how you prepare to accomplish those things. I recommend a way for golfers to move into the address position, aim, and start the backswing, but they don't have to do it my way. Fred Couples and Lee Trevino, for example, don't get up to the ball the way I do, but they both end up with E O L. They get the Form, but have their own Style of getting to it. It is a matter of what makes the individual golfer comfortable. Do you tug at your shirt the way Couples or Jack Nicklaus do when they are preparing to play a shot? Do you look at the target once, twice, three times after settling in at the ball? Do you swing relatively fast or slowly? Do you take the club back really far, past parallel, or is your backswing short by ordinary standards? All these things come under the heading of Style, and there is no one style for all golfers—and it is not important that there be. The important thing is that you end up with the Form I teach. However you come to it is your business.

Of course, I do have a method for starting the swing. It is a keystone of my teaching. But even in this you don't have to think about it, or do it as I suggest you do. I'm sure Fred Couples and Lee Trevino don't think about starting their swings the way I teach it, but that *is* what they do. On the other hand, Chi-Chi Rodriguez, Jim Albus, Larry Laoretti, and Gene Borek, among others, say that my method is an anchor for the beginning of their swing. Whether you think about that first move or not is a matter of style. Whether you actually do it or not is form. Form is what is important.

I hope that I have made it clear in this book that there is an inswing way of playing golf and a preswing way, which is what I advocate. Inswing playing has to do with thinking about what you're doing during the swing—thinking about positions and movements. I do not believe that this is the best way to play golf. I believe you play your best golf when you are not thinking at all during the swing. Even the first move, the turn of the left shoulder, is a preswing thought, although I will admit it comes very close to being inswing. The best golf swing is a reaction to how you set up to launch the ball. The left shoulder is merely the ignition key that you may, or may not, think about.

All of which is what the sports psychologists are telling players these days: that you have to be in a kind of mindless state to play well, that you can't be caught up in analysis while making a golf swing. But sports psychologists aren't giving their golfers a way to trigger the swing within that *mindless* framework. I do. Visualize the target and the type of shot you want to play; set up at the ball in a way that will insure you can do what your visualization asks, then start the left shoulder. After that, it is a non-thinking moment. In this way, the golfer can just think about his game and the shots to be played, not his swing. If a golfer doesn't adopt this methodology, he is making it hard for himself to play well. Of that I am convinced. In the course of a golf swing, which takes about a second and a half, your brain waves can't get to your body parts fast enough to influence how the body parts are going to behave. If you try to interject thoughts during that second and a half, you will slow down the physical process and progress of the swing. Slow down the process and you will mess it up, because the golf swing should be an uncontrollable act that is under control.

That last statement needs some explaining. As I've said before, the time it takes to make a golf swing is so brief that it is futile to try to shape it or reshape it once it is under way. If you do not try to influence its progress, the swing is in a sense uncontrollable; it is free of strictures and tension, which is as it should be—all the muscles and joints are allowed to work at their full capacity. That being the case, every golfer is, you might say, trapped in the motion he has created once his swing has begun. The predetermination is in the setup before the swing begins. In this way you are controlling a motion that has the capacity to be very much uncontrolled—hands and arms and legs and hips, etc., going in all directions. Those setup positions, once taken, are no longer thought about, but they effectively dictate—*control*—the swing motions that follow. When you start the left shoulder turning, you create a spinning of the upper body around its own axis or center. The swinging of the arms emanates from that coiling action, moving in an orbit controlled by muscles that are stretched or recoiling. If the left shoulder is turned to start the swing, the right shoulder can only go back. The arms can swing freely and will do so only in an orbit that has been determined by the setup positions. The arms are not being controlled while they are in motion—there is no psychological or intellectual force being put on them—but they are under control nevertheless by virtue of the positions they were in before they began their journey.

That's why, in my system, you can play golf without thinking. It is what I call being on automatic. I am offering you a system for playing golf that gives you the luxury of not thinking of your swing when you are playing. All you have to do is think of the target, set up to the ball, trigger the swing with the turn of the left shoulder, and hang on for the ride!